Victory Through Prayer!

*Carrie —
Assure Victory
Through Prayer!
BCD Mt 6:33
6/6/25*

Bill C. Dotson

Published by Bill C. Dotson
P.O. Box 195271
Dallas, Texas 75219
(214) 734-6009

ISBN: 978-0-9897398-9-4

©2024 Bill C. Dotson. All rights reserved.

No part of this book may be reproduced, stored in a retrieval system, or transmitted by any means without the written permission of the author.

Unless otherwise noted, scripture quotations are from the English Standard Version® (ESV®). Copyright ©2001 by Crossway, a publishing ministry of Good News Publishers. All rights reserved.

Scripture quotations labeled NKJV are from the New King James Version® (NKJV®). Copyright ©1982 by Thomas Nelson, Inc. Used by permission.

Scripture quotations labeled KJV are from the King James Version of the Holy Bible, 1769.

Scripture quotations labeled NIV are from the The Holy Bible, New International Version, NIV. Copyright ©1973, 1978, 1984, 2011 by Biblica, Inc. All rights reserved worldwide. Used by permission.

Printed in the United States of America by JPS Books + Logistics.

Design by Climer Design.

Dedication

This book is a testament to the love and unity of our family. It is dedicated to my wife of 65 years, Joanne, who has been my pillar of strength. To my daughters, Rebecca Ellerman and Evelyn Battaglia, who have always been my inspiration. To my grandchildren and their spouses, Luke and Meagan Ellerman, Sarah Peyton Ellerman, Annie and Wyatt D'Spain, and Renzo Battaglia, who bring joy to our lives. Also, to my great-grandchildren, Clara Louise Ellerman, Elijah Ellerman, Micah Lucas Ellerman, James D'Spain, and Lily Jane D'Spain, who are the future of our family.

A special dedication to one more grandchild, Will Daniel Ellerman. Will was born with Down Syndrome, loves the Lord passionately, and is the "chief prayer warrior" in the family.

VICTORY THROUGH PRAYER!

My Testimony About Will

Everyone in our family and beyond has their own story concerning my grandson, Will Ellerman. This is mine, and it concerns the power of prayer as it relates to Will's life.

On September 15, 1999, a baby boy was born to my oldest daughter, Rebecca Ellerman. Immediately upon birth, a code blue was pronounced at Presbyterian Hospital in Dallas. The newborn was rushed to the NICU. Everyone was in shock, and we began to pray. I and others called as many friends as possible who we knew would be praying with us. After a few hours, I got alone with the Bible and started praying to God that He would show me a verse I could claim. He led me to Psalm 27.13,14:

> "I would have lost heart, unless I had believed that I would see the goodness of the Lord in the land of the living. Wait on the Lord; be of good courage, and He shall strengthen your heart; wait, I say, on the Lord!" (NKJV)

Will Daniel Ellerman was born with Down Syndrome. He also had a hole in his heart and required a trachea to breathe as well as a feeding tube to take in nutrients. At the end of the first week, his doctors stated that he might not have a functioning brain due to a lack of oxygen. He stayed in the ICU virtually the entire first two years of his life and underwent open heart surgery at the tender age of five. He continued to need a feeding tube until he was 12.

Holy hallelujah! I am happy to report that Will is turning 25 this year and has an incredible memory for names, events, birthdays, Bible verses, and so much more. He brings so much joy to our family and everyone who knows him.

From where I sit, God honored His word because I see the goodness of the Lord in the land of the living in Will's life. It may have taken a lot of waiting initially, but God has honored it by strengthening my heart and the heart of our family. During his first two years of life, hundreds, if not thousands, of people across the country and beyond must have prayed for him.

Here's a story from that time: Once, when I was telling some people I didn't know directly about Will, one woman asked me if I was talking about Will Ellerman. I said yes. She told me she lived with her family in Grand Prairie, "and ever since we heard about him, our Sunday school class has been praying for him continually!"

What a prayer-answering God we have. I hope you look forward to reading this book. I know you have your own stories. Please share them with someone. Bring glory to God, Will is!

Foreword

Bill Dotson has a heart for the Lord, a heart for people, and a heart for eternal impact. *Victory Through Prayer!* is an outpouring of his desire to serve God and others as he unpacks the powerful yet often misunderstood discipline of prayer.

I believe every follower of Christ can stand to grow in prayer, myself included! Whether you are new to the faith or have been a believer for decades, there is always something new you can learn by abiding in and partnering with the Lord in the practice of prayer.

One verse that has struck me is Luke 2:52, which says, "And Jesus grew in wisdom and stature, and in favor with God and man" (NIV). I can't prove this, but I believe one of the ways Jesus grew in wisdom, stature, and favor is through prayer. The Gospels record multiple instances where Jesus withdrew to a quiet place to be alone with the Father and to pray. If prayer is important to Jesus, it should be important to us as well. The other striking facet of this verse is that Jesus *grew* in these things. If the Son of God can grow, we, too, should aspire to grow in our spiritual lives. One of the best ways to do that is through continuous and fervent prayer.

As the CEO of East-West, I have seen firsthand the power of prayer in the lives of the lost and unreached. Praying in the Spirit can soften the most hardened hearts in the spiritually darkest places. It can build a bridge to reach those who have never heard of Jesus. And prayer is the vessel by which unbelievers tell God they are ready to receive the free gift of salvation that Jesus offers. Prayer can literally change lives for all eternity.

Prayer increases our intimacy and dependency on God, which is why this book is so important. In it, you'll find simple truths and reminders of what prayer is, why it's essential in our lives, and how to pray by the Spirit. I pray that you will walk away from this book believing that prayer is powerful and with a greater assurance that there is, indeed, victory through prayer.

As you turn the pages of *Victory Through Prayer!*, you may discover the boundless joy, the immeasurable peace, and the unshakeable confidence that comes from knowing that you are never alone—that the God of Heaven bends His ear to hear your prayers and is always responding in His perfect goodness and sovereign power.

Blessings,
Kurt Nelson
CEO of East-West

Table of Contents

Introduction..10
Chapter 1. What is prayer?..17
Chapter 2. Where does scripture fit in?...21
Chapter 3. Why pray?..29
Testimony by Bill Lamberth..34
Testimony by Prashant Joy..36
Chapter 4. To whom do you pray?..39
Testimony by John Roper..41
Chapter 5. When do you pray?..43
Testimony by David Rodriguez...48
Testimony by Annie D'Spain..51
Chapter 6. What do you pray for?...53
Testimony by Robyn Bush...56
Chapter 7. The impact of prayer...59
Testimony by Annie Roberson...64
Chapter 8. The family prayer...67
Testimony by Dr. Jeffrey Parker..70
Chapter 9. Prayer journaling...73
Testimony by Rebecca Ellerman..76
Testimony by Sarah Peyton Ellerman..79
Chapter 10. What about fasting?..81
Testimony by Bosco Ruhinda..86
Chapter 11. Blessings and benedictions..91
Chapter 12. Before we say amen!..97
Testimony by Will Ellerman..100
Chapter 13. The gospel and prayer for salvation...............................101
Prayer Quotes..105
Seven Hebrew Words for Praise...109
Acknowledgments...110
About the Author..111

Introduction

There are thousands of books on prayer. So why am I writing this one? First, I've been encouraged by my younger daughter, Evelyn, to do so. And I, along with my other daughter, Rebecca, believe I must write it for myself and as a legacy gift to the next generations. I have yielded to the Holy Spirit; whatever He wants to write, that's what I'll attempt to do. So, here goes.

One disclaimer: *I am not a theologian, but simply a layperson who believes in the power of prayer for victorious living this side of heaven.*

My introduction to prayer was at my grandparents' dining table on special occasions. Uncle Ronald Sellers seemed to be the most faithful Christian in our family then. Whenever he was present, he would be selected to pray before the meal.

Later, as I started attending the First Baptist Church in Franklin, Tennessee, I was exposed to different types of prayers. Because I was growing up in the decade after World War II, my parents typically worked seven days a week at their family restaurant to make ends meet. I was sent to church and instructed to stay for the church service, not just Sunday School. Well, that's when I learned my first personal prayers to God. The Baptist preacher was always discussing hellfire and damnation, a frightening experience for a pre-teen. On Sunday nights, when I got into bed, I remember praying desperately that neither God nor the devil would harm me for all the bad things I knew I was doing, many of which the preacher was talking about.

As God would have it, my mother decided to leave work and come to church with me one Sunday morning. I usually sat in the back row, scared to death of the message, but we decided to sit down in front. When the preacher called for anyone (re)dedicating their life to Christ to come forward, my mother did so, and I followed her bravely. She rededicated her life to Jesus that day, and I trusted Jesus in the best way possible as a 12-year-old. I was subsequently baptized and started my Christian journey.

INTRODUCTION

After that, no one specifically taught me anything about prayer. I learned it through osmosis, watching teachers and other church members pray. I didn't read any books or study prayer intentionally. God was mostly someone who could help me when I desperately needed it. Looking back now, I was at least reaching out to God and beginning some form of prayer life, even if it was selfish. I think God's grace started showing up early in my prayer life.

Moving forward, as a young person, I was most likely reciting nursery rhyme prayers such as, "Now I lay me down to sleep, I pray the Lord my soul to keep. If I should die before I wake, I pray the Lord my soul to take." But it was a start. And thankfully, I grew from there. I constantly and desperately prayed about grades, athletics, friendships, and all those mean bullies in my school. (I was small and always picked on!) Then, as I "matured" in my Christian walk, I started praying about dating girls. You know, big stuff!

Meeting Joanne Paschall (my wife of 65 years) intensified my prayer life—especially as I considered asking her to marry me. I didn't know how to put things in the hands of God. I still wanted Him to meet my needs, whatever they might be. I must not have done it all wrong, as Joanne said yes. As in this case, God's grace is always at work in our prayer life. I take great comfort in the words of Paul:

> *"Likewise, the Spirit helps us in our weakness. For we do not know what to pray for as we ought, but the Spirit himself intercedes for us with groanings too deep for words. And he who searches hearts knows what is the mind of the Spirit, because the Spirit intercedes for the saints according to the will of God"* (Rom. 8:26,27).

Once I was married, helping raise two children, and working in a career with more responsibilities than ever, I found much more reason to have a productive prayer life. I must admit that although I was a nominal Christian, I had a less-than-nominal prayer life. But pray, I did, as best I knew how. Still, I didn't understand completely the meaning of grace. In hindsight, however, I see that grace was always at work.

I also didn't understand the process of prayer. I only knew that my family and I had needs and wants and that God was the best source to turn to. I was truly an amateur, mainly praying at meals and bedtime with our daughters.

In my early 30s, after moving to Dallas from Nashville for work in real estate, my career turned upside down due to a strong recession. Ever a faithful heavenly Father, God took me to my knees. I prayed: "God, take out of my life what's standing between you and me." When I stood up; my life's never been the same. The following morning, Joanne gave me a book by Keith Miller called *The Taste of New Wine*. It was so powerful! She also shared that she and her Christian women friends had been praying for me. I can honestly say to you the word of God started leaping off the page. I had been "born again" or "Spirit-filled." Only God knows. Praise Him!

The word of God became so real and personal. Spiritual and Biblical messages were becoming more apparent. I started to trust His word prayerfully and try to follow His commandments as best I could. My prayer life took a giant leap forward. I began to understand that the scripture teaches that we pray to the Father in the power of the Holy Spirit and in the name of Jesus. I realized that Jesus was our Great High Priest, our Chief Intercessor before the Father. That opened my eyes even more to the need for— and the power of—prayer.

One of the most wonderful things was happening. I was seeing many of my prayers being answered specifically. The Lord's Prayer became my model. Matthew 6:33 and 34, which talk about seeking Him first, became my life verses. This led me to begin each day in a "quiet time" with the Lord—like a prayer closet! It has been one of my greatest joys ever since. It is personal and powerful!

One of the most influential men in my prayer life is E. M. Bounds (1835 to 1913). He is known for writing eleven books, nine focused on prayer. We'll talk more about him later. Another significant impact on my prayer life was praying before the 2008 presidential elections with about 70 people at the Washington Monument. We were given 20 minutes to share openly what was on our hearts. An African American pastor from Washington, D.C., delivered his comments on prayer. After he was through, we thanked him for such a powerful message. For some reason, he looked straight at me and said, "Bill, you do know that God runs His universe and kingdom through the prayers of His people, don't you?" It hit me like a ton of bricks and opened my eyes to

INTRODUCTION

how God values the prayers of His people and wants to hear them. It's like a partnership with the Trinity.

One of the prayer-altering takeaways from that encounter is the message in the book of Ephesians. I want you to imagine with me this fact: If you are a born-again believer, your soul is already "in Christ." And because Christ is seated in heaven at the right hand of the Father, interceding to the Father through prayers, pleadings, and supplications, would it not make sense that you and I are there with him, "in him"? The Spirit orchestrated all of this for us and in us. The following verses reveal these truths.

First, read this passage:

> *"And what is the immeasurable greatness of his power toward us who believe, according to the working of his great might that he worked in Christ when he raised him from the dead and seated him at his right hand in the heavenly places, far above all rule and authority and power and dominion, and above every name that is named, not only in this age but also in the one to come"* (Eph. 1:19-21).

Now, reflect on this:

> *"Even when we were dead in our trespasses, made us alive together with Christ—by grace you have been saved—and raised us up with him and seated us with him in the heavenly places in Christ Jesus, so that in the coming ages he might show the immeasurable riches of his grace in kindness toward us in Christ Jesus"* (Eph. 2:5-7).

That experience showed me how personal and intimate our relationship with God is and that when we are in prayer, we are spiritually seated right there with the Trinity, "in Christ," addressing the things of their kingdom and universe. Thank you, D.C. pastor!

Another "aha moment" in the development of my prayer life came when my mother had a major operation and was recovering. As I called her each day, I could detect how she was feeling from her voice. One day, she seemed different—brighter and more cheerful. I asked her what was behind the change.

She answered, "Most people who come by or call say they are or will be praying for me. But last night, my next-door neighbors, retired missionaries, visited and prayed over me. It made all the difference."

What I learned and have implemented from that day forward is this: When someone is in need or asks for prayers, do it right then, in person, over the phone, by text or email, whatever. The Holy Spirit ministers to that person—and you—right then. It is so much more effective than putting the prayers off, for we often forget.

A recent public confession of sin, read in unison during our church service, touched my heart significantly. It spoke to me about the power of the gospel in prayer. I want to share it with you here:

> *"Oh Lord, no day of my life has passed*
> > *that has not proved me guilty of sin.*
> *Prayers have been uttered from a prayerless heart;*
> > *praise has been often praiseless sound.*
> *Lord Jesus, though my sins rise to heaven*
> > *Your merits soar above them.*
> *I appeal from the throne of Your perfect justice*
> > *to Your throne of boundless grace.*
> *Grant me to hear Your voice assuring me that I am*
> > *guilty of sin, but pardoned;*
> > *wandering, but found;*
> > *sinning, but cleansed.*
> *Give me a perpetual broken heartedness,*
> > *keep me always clinging to Your cross,*
> > *flood me every moment with descending grace."*

Several years ago, I was encouraged by the prayer that Ramesh Richard, founder of RREACH ministries and professor at Dallas Seminary, received from his father who had created a daily prayer for his family and continued to pray over his family for 30 years.

I began to pray over scripture about what God wanted me to pray daily for my family. My family now includes my wife, two daughters, five grandchildren

INTRODUCTION

(two married), and five great-grandchildren. Later in the book, I will reveal it to you. Maybe it will inspire you to prayerfully create your own.

While developing my personal prayer discipline, I found it to be scripturally sound doctrine to pray in agreement with others. That could be with your spouse, your children, your extended family, or your brothers or sisters in Christ.

Reflect on Jesus' words:

> *"Truly, I say to you, whatever you bind on earth shall be bound in heaven, and whatever you loose on earth shall be loosed in heaven. Again I say to you, if two of you agree on earth about anything they ask, it will be done for them by my Father in heaven. For where two or three are gathered in my name, there am I among them"* (Mt. 18:18-20).

Two decades ago, I had the privilege of sitting with a couple of other people under the teaching of Clyde J. Hodson, author of the PrayerMentor Booklet Series *Coming* to a *Place of Abiding*. It's the first and probably the only time I have ever explicitly studied under someone about how to pray, the value of prayer, and so much more. I discovered the value of group prayers, regular prayer meetings, prayer walks, and other means of prayer.

For a long time, I had never understood or even thought about the meaning of "Amen." I just knew that you were supposed to say that at the end of a prayer. Obviously, it must be important. I learned that it meant, among other things, "so be it," or "may it be so," or even "agree with" or "confirm." I prefer the terminology "let it be done." To me, saying "amen" is an act of faith, believing confidently that God hears and will answer in His own time according to His will.

Praying, journaling, fasting…so much can be involved in your prayer life. It's a daily mindset. Jesus is our best model. Studying his three-year ministry here on Earth will show that prayer was so vital to Him that He would only do what He saw or heard the Father show Him. I challenge you to do the same. Let's grow in our prayer life together.

The apostle Paul revealed that we are to pray without ceasing. And that the prayers of a righteous person avail much. I'll leave you with these exhortations.

> *"Rejoice always, pray without ceasing, give thanks in all circumstances; for this is the will of God in Christ Jesus for you"* (I Thess.5:16-18).

> *"The prayer of a righteous person has great power as it is working"* (James 5:16b).

One final thought: The Lord requires and loves the first fruits of our labors, financially and otherwise. As your day begins, your prayer life with the Lord is the precious first fruits. Give Him all you can.

I'll let E. M. Bounds close us. To men and women!

> *"Few Christians have anything but a vague idea of the power of prayer; fewer still have any experience of that power. The Church seems almost wholly unaware of the power God puts into her hand; this spiritual carte blanche on the infinite resources of God's wisdom and power is rarely, if ever, used—never used to the full measure of honouring God."*

I could go on reflecting, but I believe we need to move into the major elements of prayer and how prayer can change your life and the world around you.

Are you ready for this prayer journey and discovering how there is *victory through prayer?*

Chapter 1
What is prayer?

As recorded in Genesis 1 and 2, God walked about in His creation, having a relationship with that which He had created, especially with Adam and then Eve. He had commanded them about the two types of trees, one providing life, the other bringing death. God gave Adam four additional commands: procreate, fill the Earth, subdue it, and have dominion. He also told Adam that He had given him every herb that yields seed on the face of all the Earth and every green herb for food. In addition, God gave Adam the authority to name everything, even the woman who was taken from his body. This scripture shows us that Adam and Eve communicated directly and personally with God.

Then comes Genesis 3 and the original sin. Through the temptation and their disobedience by eating the fruit of the forbidden tree, sin was introduced. Sin is, in effect, separation from God. But before removing them from paradise, God came looking for them, as if He didn't know where they were, and spoke with them. Adam spoke back to God about their shame. Again, personal communication. After God pronounced their punishment, they had, as we do, a broken relationship with God, which only Jesus can redeem.

So, how does prayer come into play in all of this? God, in His grace and mercy, provided a way for sinful people to communicate with him. Prayer is that means of communication. So, prayer was introduced for fellowship and relationship with the God of the universe. He made a way for His created beings to speak with Him and He with them. Today, we know this is brought about by the Spirit of God, who dwells in each believer.

The Old and New Testaments speak of prayer in many ways and under many conditions. The patriarchs, prophets, apostles, and believers were all desperate to pray. One has only to read the Psalms, which are, for the most part, prayerful songs. They deal with every emotion and circumstance imaginable. No one prayer fits all. But I find it interesting that the disciples asked Jesus how to pray early on. They saw John the Baptist and Jesus bathing their lives in prayer. And they saw many miracles.

Jesus presented the disciples with the model prayer, which we know as the Lord's Prayer. It is the framework for all our prayers.

> *"Pray then like this: 'Our Father in heaven, hallowed be your name. Your kingdom come, your will be done, on earth as it is in heaven. Give us this day our daily bread, and forgive us our debts, as we also have forgiven our debtors. And lead us not into temptation, but deliver us from evil'"* (Mt. 6:9-13).

Over time, many began adding the following sentence, found in some early manuscripts: *"For yours is the kingdom and the power and the glory forever. Amen."*

Throughout my life, I have been introduced to several acronyms for prayer designed to remind us how to pray. Here are just a few. You could create your own as well.

PRAY   Praise, Repent, Ask, Yield

ACTS   Adoration, Confession, Thanksgiving, Supplication

PRAISE   Praise, Repentance, Ask, Intercede, Speak the Word, Enjoy His presence

All the words in these acronyms reflect the multi-faceted breadth and depth of prayer. When, where, and the content of your prayer varies in every circumstance. One of the oft-quoted and possibly all-time-misunderstood verses is in I Thessalonians 5.17. *"Pray without ceasing."* This passage is not calling us to be monks praying ceaselessly in a cave. As we go about our lives, we face many opportunities and challenges. I believe we are instead called to have a prayerful attitude, forever ready to lift a form of prayer in whatever circumstance we or others are facing. Paul also says to "rejoice always and to give thanks in all circumstances." Doing so keeps God in control as we are only the vessels for these prayers.

Prayer is an intimate partnership with our friend, the Lord.

CHAPTER 1 - WHAT IS PRAYER?

> *"No longer do I call you servants, for the servant does not know what his master is doing; but I have called you friends, for all that I have heard from my Father I have made known to you"* (John 15:15).

Pause right now and wrap your mind around the fact that Jesus Christ, who laid down His life for you, for me, and for the body of Christ, calls us His friends. Wow! That means that prayer is simply friends sharing with each other the issues in the world, in our hearts, and in the kingdom of God. How much more intimate can it get? That's what prayer provides and is. This awesome idea is amplified throughout scripture.

And that leads us to the fact that prayer is so critical to…*abiding*. Among other things, abiding means *dwelling constantly* and *being present*. There are no more significant or more evident passages in all scripture concerning abiding than John 15:1-12—the thesis on abiding. I want you to read it, meditate on it, and see the fruitfulness of abiding in Christ.

Here's one of the verses to get you started:

> *"If you abide in me, and my words abide in you, ask whatever you wish, and it will be done for you. By this my Father is glorified, that you bear much fruit and so prove to be my disciples"* (vv.7,8). I'm sure you noticed the word ask. That's prayer! And a vital part of abiding.

This leads us to the next chapter, which addresses prayer and scripture.

VICTORY THROUGH PRAYER!

Chapter 2
Where does scripture fit in?

The quick, simple answer is…*everywhere!* As I have grown in my love for and a better understanding of prayer, it has become abundantly clear that God has given us a prayer textbook—the Holy Bible. If you want to offer praise, go to the Psalms. If you want to strengthen your faith through prayer, meditate on the lives of the many people that appear from Genesis to Revelation. Many of Paul's letters include prayers. And Paul reminds his disciples and readers that he has continually prayed for them.

I would say that the Bible is one massive prayer, from start to finish. Some parts might not seem like prayers, but God's will for His people here on Earth is available 24/7 through the reading of scripture. He loves hearing His thoughts provided throughout scripture, His truth spoken back by His "friends." Think about how you feel when someone quotes what you said earlier because your words impacted their life. It most likely brought joy to your heart. That's scripture being prayed in spades.

I love II Timothy 3:16,17.

> *"All Scripture is breathed out by God and profitable for teaching, for reproof, for correction, and for training in righteousness, that the man of God may be complete, equipped for every good work."*

This passage tells us that using scripture in prayer expresses the "breathed out" word, the inspired word of God, with all its power and strength. Following this prayer model will not return void. You are not just babbling empty phrases; you are putting God's powerful truths and promises into action. Think of the Bible as your prayer "script" (as in scripture!).

Scripture is the best place to learn *how* to pray and know *what* to pray. It tells us that we can draw near to God through prayer, bring Him our requests, ask for His help, and He will meet us in times of need. You can even speak scripture about prayer back to God when you don't know what to pray. These verses will encourage your daily walk with Christ and help you experience the power of prayer!

There are far too many examples to include here, but the following selections will help emphasize the importance of quoting scripture in prayer.

- "Do not be anxious about anything, but in everything by prayer and supplication with thanksgiving let your requests be made known unto God. And the peace of God, which surpasses all understanding, will guard your hearts and your minds in Christ Jesus" (Phil. 4:6,7).

- "I say to the Lord, you are my God; give ear to the voice of my pleas for mercy, O Lord! O Lord, my Lord, the strength of my salvation, you have covered my head in the day of battle. Grant not, O Lord, the desires of the wicked; do not further their evil plot, or they will be exalted!" (Psa. 140:6-8).

- "Therefore I tell you, whatever you ask in prayer, believe that you have received it, and it will be yours. And whenever you stand praying, forgive, if you have anything against anyone, so that your Father also who is in heaven may forgive you your trespasses" (Mark 11:24-26).

- Likewise the Spirit helps us in our weakness. For we do not know what to pray for as we ought, but the Spirit himself intercedes for us with groanings too deep for words" (Rom. 8:26).

- "Therefore, confess your sins to one another and pray for one another, that you may be healed. The prayer of a righteous person has great power as it is working" (James 5:16).

- "Rejoice always, pray without ceasing, give thanks in all circumstances; for this is the will of God in Christ Jesus for you" (I Thess. 5:16-18).

- "This is the confidence we have toward him, that if we ask anything according to his will he hears us. And if we know that he hears us in whatever we ask, we know that we have the request that we have asked of him" (I John 5:14,15).

- "If my people who are called by my name humble themselves, and pray and seek my face and turn from their wicked ways, then I will hear from heaven and will forgive their sin and heal their land" (II Chron. 7:14).

- "Praying at all times in the Spirit, with all prayer and supplication. To that end, keep alert with all perseverance, making supplication for all the saints" (Eph. 6:18).

CHAPTER 2 - WHERE DOES SCRIPTURE FIT IN?

- *"The Lord is my shepherd; I shall not want. He makes me lie down in green pastures. He leads me beside still waters. He restores my soul. He leads me in paths of righteousness for his name's sake. Even though I walk through the valley of the shadow of death, I will fear no evil, for you are with me; your rod and your staff, they comfort me. You prepare a table before me in the presence of my enemies; you anoint my head with oil; my cup overflows. Surely goodness and mercy shall follow me all the days of my life, and I shall dwell in the house of the Lord forever"* (Psa. 23).

- *"For this reason, because I have heard of your faith in the Lord Jesus and your love toward all the saints, I do not cease to give thanks for you, remembering you in my prayers, that the God of our Lord Jesus Christ, the Father of glory, may give you the Spirit of wisdom and revelation in the knowledge of him, having the eyes of your hearts enlightened, that you may know what is the hope to which he has called you, what are the riches of his glorious inheritance in the saints, and what is the immeasurable greatness of his power toward us who believe, according to the working of his great might that he worked in Christ when he raised him from the dead and seated him at his right hand in the heavenly places, far above all rule and authority and power and dominion, and above every name with that is named, not only in this age but also in the age to come"* (Eph. 1:15-21).

This is only a small sampling of prayers within scripture. The Bible is filled with prayers. All the biblical leaders knew the importance of prayer. They prayed for blessings, healing, family, strength, understanding, direction, unbelievers, and so much more.

The following are a few additional passages that have helped in my own prayer life. Most are from Psalms, which is always a good source of prayerful quotes.

- *"Make me to know your ways, O Lord; teach me your paths. Lead me in your truth and teach me, for you are the God of my salvation; for you I wait all the day long. Remember your mercy, O Lord, and your steadfast love, for they have been from old. Remember not the sins of my youth or my transgressions; according to your steadfast love remember me, for the sake of your goodness, O Lord"* (Psa. 25:4-7).

- *"Search me, O God, and know my heart! Try me and know my thoughts!*

And see if there be any grievous way in me, and lead me in the way everlasting" (Psa. 139:23,24).

- *"My soul melts away for sorrow; strengthen me according to your word! Put false ways far from me and graciously teach me your law"* (Psa. 119:28,29).

- *Heal me, O Lord, and I shall be healed; save me, and I shall be saved, for you are my praise"* (Jer. 17:14).

Also from Psalms is a prayer of David after it was disclosed to him that his sins had been made public and God was aware of his waywardness. Once Nathan rebuked and exhorted him, David's cry to the Lord in Psalm 51 is a prayer for all times, and for all sinners. We have all been in his position and may even be there now. I will only share a couple of verses, but I invite you to read them, pray about them, and meditate on them.

"Have mercy on me, O God, according to your steadfast love; according to your abundant mercy blot out my transgressions. Wash me thoroughly from my iniquity, and cleanse me from my sin!... Purge me with hyssop, and I shall be clean; wash me, and I will be whiter than snow... Create in me a clean heart, O God, and renew a right spirit within me. Cast me not away from your presence, and take not your Holy Spirit from me. Restore to me the joy of your salvation, and uphold me with a willing spirit (vv.1,2,7,10-12).

I've always found this prayer to be doubly powerful. After David confesses and cries out to God for mercy, he then commits to be one of God's evangelists. His sins were so convicting, and his prayer was so sincere and humble. David saw the need to spread the truth about God—all within one prayer:

"Then I will teach transgressors your ways, and sinners will return to you. Deliver me from blood guiltiness, O God, O God of my salvation, and my tongue will sing aloud of your righteousness. O Lord, open my lips, and my mouth will declare your praise" (vv.13-15).

Then David, through the Spirit, prays what God truly desires from us:

"For you will not delight in sacrifice, or I would give it; you will not be

> *pleased with a burnt offering. The sacrifices of God are a broken spirit;*
> *a broken and contrite heart, O God, you will not despise"* (vv.16,17).

As we can see, while prayer is about a lot of things, it is primarily about us and our relationship with God. After receiving salvation based on the justification of the cross, we enter into an immediate period of sanctification until we meet Christ face to face. Prayer is the one place where we get honest before God, either privately or corporately, and He changes us, making us into the image of Christ.

God has an amazing plan for every one of His children. Peter reveals what God is doing with us and that prayer is the vehicle through which most of this occurs. What we are to become is worked out mostly through His word and through prayer. In other words, you are what you pray!

> *"As you come to him, a living stone rejected by men but in the sight of God chosen and precious, you yourselves like living stones are being built up as a spiritual house, to be a holy priesthood, to offer spiritual sacrifices acceptable to God through Jesus Christ… But you are a chosen race, a royal priesthood, a holy nation, a people for his own possession, that you may proclaim the excellencies of him who called you out of darkness into his marvelous light. Once you were not a people, but now you are God's people; once you had not received mercy, but now you have received mercy"* (I Peter 2:4,5,9-10).

Prayer touches every phase of our lives, as do the scriptures. When you combine prayer with scripture, you invoke God's omnipotent, omniscient, and omnipresent character. Nothing can equal it. Scriptural prayer assures victory. God loves it, and you can be assured He will honor it.

I find it so interesting that after we disobeyed God, turned our backs on Him, and became His enemies, what did He do? He provided a sacrifice for us in His Son on Golgotha, and He provided prayer and the necessary truth (His word) that we would need to be victorious in this life and beyond. What an awesome God we serve.

It is essential to understand that prayer is only effective when offered in humility. Not without boldness and assurance, but humbly.

- *"Humble yourselves, therefore, under the mighty hand of God so that at the proper time he may exalt you, casting all your anxieties on him, because he cares for you"* (I Peter 5:6,7).

- *"But he gives more grace. Therefore it says, 'God opposes the proud but gives grace to the humble'"* (James 4:6).

The humble mindset of Jesus is another powerful testimony:

"Have this mind among yourselves, which is yours in Christ Jesus, who, though he was in the form of God, did not count equality with God a thing to be grasped, but emptied himself, by taking the form of a servant, being born in the likeness of men. And being found in human form, he humbled himself by becoming obedient to the point of death, even death on a cross" (Phil. 2:8).

Jesus' humility was never more present than when praying to the Father in the Garden of Gethsemane the night before His crucifixion. This is our prayer mindset model for all times:

"And he withdrew from them about a stone's throw, and knelt down and prayed, saying, 'Father, if you are willing, remove this cup from me. Nevertheless, not my will, but yours, be done'" (Luke 22:41,42).

And see what His Father did at that very moment in response to His obedience and humility:

And there appeared to him an angel from heaven, strengthening him" (v.43).

It is easy to pass over this scripture and not grasp the magnitude of this moment in time that secured salvation for all who believe. Lean into this:

"And being in agony he prayed more earnestly; and his sweat became like great drops of blood falling down to the ground" (v.44).

Considering the circumstances, I find this last action on Jesus' part to be simply incredible:

> *"And when he rose from prayer, he came to the disciples and found them sleeping for sorrow, and he said to them, 'Why are you sleeping? Rise and pray that you may not enter into temptation'"* (vv.45,46).

Will we be found sleeping, or will we be vigilant in prayer, knowing that prayer assures victory? This next prayer by Jesus, who is being crucified and hanging on a cross, bleeding and suffocating, is one for all eternity:

> *"And Jesus said, 'Father, forgive them, for they know not what they do'"* (Luke 23: 34).

Finally, Jesus' last prayer from the cross revealed His complete, indisputable confidence in His Father.

> *"Then Jesus, calling out with a loud voice, said, 'Father, into your hands I commit my spirit!'"* (v.46).

Are you ready to pray to the Father with this level of assurance? Start by quoting these last passages—and practice, practice, practice.

VICTORY THROUGH PRAYER!

Chapter 3
Why pray?

"Why" may be the most important question to answer. Because, as the following scriptures point out, we here are in a spiritual battle, played out in countless ways in our lives, and in the world. The enemies are our flesh, the world's trappings, and Satan himself. So, the most powerful weapon we have, along with God's word, is prayer. As I say to many fathers, "It's the most important tool in your toolbox."

> *"Finally, be strong in the Lord and in the strength of his might. Put on the whole armor of God, that you may be able to stand against the schemes of the devil. For we do not wrestle against flesh and blood, but against the rulers, against the authorities, against the cosmic powers over this present darkness, against the spiritual forces of evil in the heavenly places. Therefore take up the whole armor of God, that you may be able to withstand in the evil day, and having done all, to stand firm. Stand therefore, having fastened on the belt of truth, and having put on the breastplate of righteousness, and, as shoes for your feet, having put on the readiness given by the gospel of peace. In all circumstances take up the shield of faith, with which you can extinguish all the flaming darts of the evil one; and take the helmet of salvation, and the sword of the Spirit, which is the word of God, praying at all times in the Spirit, with all prayer and supplication. To that end, keep alert with all perseverance, making supplication for all the saints, and also for me, that words may be given to me in opening my mouth boldly to proclaim the mystery of the gospel, for which I am an ambassador in chains, that I may declare it boldly, as I ought to speak"* (Eph. 6:10-20).

Throughout my life, I have heard numerous people express their disbelief in or question whether prayer works. So many of us pray for our loved ones to get well, and then they die. Maybe this sounds familiar: *"I prayed that my daddy wouldn't die, but he did. So why should I pray since God didn't do that for me?"* It is evident that a majority of people, especially non-Christians, don't understand the sovereignty of God. He has given us free will to obey or disobey, trust or not trust, serve or not serve, worship or not worship. But, for the most part, selfish humankind wants *"MY will be done."*

Often, the problem stems from a misunderstanding of the purpose of prayer. If it's only to get your way, you will be disappointed. Or your attitude might be, "God already knows everything that will happen, so why should I bother praying? What good would that do?" However, praying is not about always getting/receiving; it's about being in a relationship. Nothing is more intimate with the Lord of creation and His created beings, you and me, than prayer—communing with the living God! Pause and think about that. We simply need it as His children, His treasured possession.

> *"O Lord, you have searched me and known me! You know when I sit down and when I rise up; you discern my thoughts from afar. You search out my path and my lying down and are acquainted with all my ways. Even before a word is on my tongue, behold, O Lord, you know it all together. You hem me in, behind and before, and lay your hand upon me. Such knowledge is too wonderful for me; it is high; I cannot attain it"* (Psa. 139:1-4).

We certainly will never be able to attain it because *His thoughts are higher than our thoughts, and His ways are higher than our ways*, but prayer allows us to pursue it, to get a close-up view of who He is and what His plan is for our life and those close to us. You and I don't know what will happen in the very next second. You don't know what's around the corner, over the hill, down the road, and so on. Yet prayer provides faith and hope to move out victoriously, even without knowing the outcome. It provides us with confidence in our Lord. Our prayers transition from talking to Him *to* talking *with* Him.

This is where faith comes in.

> *"Now faith is the assurance of things hoped for, the conviction of things not seen"* (Heb. 11:1).

Our prayers must be bathed in faith to be heard.

> *"And without faith it is impossible to please him, for whoever would*

draw near to God must believe that he exists and that he rewards those who seek him" (v. 6).

We must understand and believe that Jesus is our Intercessor, seated at the right hand of the Father. He faced what you and I face every day while He was here on Earth. If Jesus the man prayed, then we must also, and with faith. We must also understand that prayer is not wishful thinking that God will do everything we ask, but assurance that He hears and will answer our prayers at the right time and in the way that will glorify Him and bless you/us and others.

Trust in God—He hears and intercedes!

> *"In the days of his flesh, Jesus offered up prayers and supplications, with loud cries and tears, to him who is able to save him from death and he was heard because of his reverence. Although he was a son, he learned obedience through what he suffered. And being made perfect, he became the source of eternal salvation to all who obey him, being designated by God a high priest after the order of Melchizedek"* (Heb. 5:7-10).

I have found that, over time, you learn to recognize God's voice as He speaks to you. It may not be audible, but you know it's Him. God uses prayer to transform our hearts, so fulfilling our request becomes secondary to feeling truly known by God and precious to Him.

We all want to lead a victorious life, and believers want to be one of the victors in God's kingdom work here on Earth. Here's a helpful analogy: A few years back, the Houston Astros won the World Series, only they won it by stealing the signals of the other team's manager with an outfield camera and, therefore, knew what pitch or decision was being made beforehand. Of course, they still had to execute the plays even though they had that knowledge. Prayer is very similar, though not in an illegal manner. We get to know in advance what our chief enemy in the world will most likely do and what his plans are. But most importantly, we know what our Lord can and will do and what His plans are. We WIN!!

Years ago, our real estate firm employed a deaf gentleman who had played football for Southern Methodist University during its glory days. He shared that in one game while playing defense, he started interpreting the verbal signals the opposing coaches called from the sideline and passed them on to his teammates. Prayer is like this. We get to know in advance what will happen, that God will call the right play, and, by faith, we can act appropriately and be victorious.

So, why pray? Here are a few of my observations. I'm sure you have many more. Dwell on them. Share them with your family and your brothers and sisters in Christ.

Prayer:

- leads to developing an intimate personal relationship with the living God
- deepens your understanding of who God is and who you are
- provides humility and reverence
- is the proving ground for faith, hope, and love
- cultivates your heart, preparing it for victorious living
- offers peace to your heart, mind, and soul
- is the safest place to express your innermost feelings without fear of condemnation.

Praying allows you to:

- rejoice in sorrows and triumphs
- see God's will be done when praying specifically
- get answers and see God's footprints when looking back
- know whether it is time to be still or move forward.
- gain the confidence to face the unknown with boldness and courage.

Why pray? Because it is where everything begins and ends. So, pray we shall! Right?

CHAPTER 3 - WHY PRAY?

Note: It has become clear to me over the years that God only hears one prayer from a nonbeliever. And that prayer is…the prayer of repentance and faith in Jesus for their salvation. At that point, the Holy Spirit becomes involved, and the infinite resources of God are now available to that person, a new child of God, *a new creation*. And prayer is one of those incredible resources. If you are reading this as someone who has never trusted Christ alone for their salvation, I invite you to go to the chapter entitled "The gospel and prayer for salvation" starting on page 101. I pray that this will be the day you trust Christ as your Savior.

Testimony by Bill Lamberth

Pastor of Young Families Ministry, Park Cities Presbyterian Church, Dallas, Texas

What's in your cup?

And He said, "Abba, Father, all things are possible for you. Remove this cup from me. Yet not what I will, but what you will" (Mark 14:36).

The call came in midafternoon on a gloomy January day. The police officer said, "Your wife has been in a car accident, and they are taking her to the hospital." So began a five-day journey of highs and lows, of many, many prayers. Not just mine, but the prayers of countless friends and family, who were pleading with God to spare my wife.

But on a Sunday, my lovely bride of only three years died.

How do we deal with prayers that are seemingly unanswered? How does it affect our relationship with God Himself? Although our situations are hard to compare with the experience of Jesus as He prayed that long night in the garden, we nevertheless ask that God would remove this cup from us. My prayer was that God would remove the cup of my wife's impending death from me. But God's will was not my will. How do I possibly move forward?

When I was a child, my parents taught me the simple children's prayer: "God is great, God is good, let us thank Him for our food." In retrospect, this prayer is far from simple. "God is great" implies His great power, His majesty, His glory. "God is good" describes His nature, that He can be trusted, and He has your very best interests at heart. "Let us thank Him for our food" describes the desired trajectory of grateful hearts as we receive His gracious providence.

It was the second of these profound statements that sustained me during those dark and lonely days. God is good. I held that reality close. God is good and He can be trusted. He has my very best interests at heart. He loves me even when His answer to my prayer is different than I had wished. His will was evidently different from mine. But God sustained me through the provision of loving friends who came around me and held me up by their constant presence. I did not eat a meal by myself for six months.

Several years later I was reminded of God's goodness and His kind provision. The doctors were able to use my wife's corneas to give sight to someone else. God used her death to answer the prayer of another person, a prayer for sight. I once told this to a work colleague, who replied that he had undergone a cornea transplant. He said, "I am humbled that someone had to die in order for me to see."

How do we go forward when God's will is different from ours? We hold tight to the loving goodness of God. We trust that He has our very best interests at heart. God is good and does good. He can be trusted even when our prayers are seemingly unanswered.

"Not my will, but Thy will."

Testimony by Prashant Joy
Technology Consultant and Servant Leader

"Often in our lives, our sense of hope is dependent on our circumstances, but no matter what the season and trials we are going through, this is not true for children of the living God (Psa. 33:20-22)."

As a family, we have been on a journey with our younger son's health challenges for the last eight-plus years. We have multiple issues to deal with daily, as well as the pressures of our son's ongoing care, as his condition requires lifelong management. We start each morning with a medical procedure that lasts about an hour or longer. Otherwise, our days are highly unpredictable, including rushing to the ER multiple times—often when we have an important work meeting or presentation we cannot miss.

In the last few years, the spiritual warfare and trials have increased on several fronts. My wife had to take multiple overseas trips due to her mom's hospitalization, and my dad was also hospitalized for extended periods. As a couple, we also had to manage our jobs, our older son and his needs, and the continual medical care for our younger son. We were physically, spiritually, and provision-wise stretched and burning out.

Earlier this year, my mother-in-law—who was a strong prayer warrior in our lives—passed away, and subsequently, my father passed away while I was holding his hands and praying over him.

Suddenly, as a husband, father, son, brother, peer, friend, and leader at work, I felt completely knocked off my feet and was struggling even to raise myself up physically, emotionally, and spiritually. In my utter despair, brokenness, and helplessness, and not knowing how to move forward, I turned to the one thing that the LORD has put on my heart to do at all times: Pray, Pray, and Pray (1Thess. 5:16-18). And when there was no energy left to pray, I just whispered to the LORD and cried out to HIM knowing HE hears and HE answers (Psa. 116:1-2).

Prayer was and is integral to our lives. The LORD has put it on my heart to pray and for my wife and me to come together to specifically pray for oneness and joy in our lives at all times and in all seasons, and that prayer should be our first response, not last.

In the past, before realizing the importance of prayer and the sheer joy it brings in pouring out our hearts and casting all our cares to the LORD, any trial in our lives would have easily led to a season of anger, bitterness, isolation, arguments, or outbursts in our family. But the LORD has changed it and made trials to be all the more an opportunity to pray, worship, soak in the word, and absolutely surrender to the LORD, for the LORD will indeed fight our battles (Ex. 14:14—The LORD will fight your battles, all you need to do is be still).

Dear Reader, no matter where you are today, God has a purpose for you and your life; it is never too difficult for our LORD to restore you and your life, no matter how hopeless and helpless you feel.

Ephesians 6:12 says, "For our struggle is not against flesh and blood, but against the rulers, against the authorities, against the powers of this dark world and against the spiritual forces of evil in the heavenly realms."

Even during dark, trying times, you are not alone. Exercise the prayer muscle consistently and make it your first resort at all times, for our God can be trusted. HE will not fail, HE will come to your rescue, and HE will heal, HE will restore, HE will do unimaginable and wonderful things in your life, for HE is already writing a story through our lives for HIS Glory. Amen!

VICTORY THROUGH PRAYER!

Chapter 4
To whom do you pray?

The short and simple answer is God. But the true answer is much more complex. Scripture shows us that the three persons of the Godhead—Father, Son, and Holy Spirit—are all involved. I think it is critical that we clearly understand their plan for victorious prayer. Let's start with Jesus' words while on Earth.

> *"If you love me, you will keep my commandments. And I will ask the Father, and he will give you another Helper, to be with you forever, even the Spirit of truth, whom the world cannot receive, because it neither sees him nor knows him. You know him, for he dwells with you and will be in you"* (John 14:16,17).

What we see here is the Holy Trinity. Jesus, the Son, will ask the Father to give you a Helper, the Holy Spirit. We get a glimpse of the relationship that will play out in our prayer methodology. And then we are told this by Jesus:

> *"You did not choose me, but I chose you and appointed you that you should go and bear fruit and that your fruit should abide, so that whatever you ask the Father in my name, he may give it to you"* (John 15:16).

Further, we see one of the primary roles of the Holy Spirit in our prayer life. Paul, writing to the Romans in the power of the Holy Spirit, shares the following with us:

> *"Likewise the Spirit helps us in our weakness. For we do not know what to pray for as we ought, but the Spirit himself intercedes for us with groanings too deep for words. And he who searches hearts knows what is the mind of the Spirit, because the Spirit intercedes for the saints according to the will of God"* (Rom. 8:26,27).

As creation and believers both groan for ultimate restoration, the Spirit does as well. He utters divine articulations within the Trinity that cannot be expressed in words but carry profound appeals for the welfare of every believer and the created world. This work of the Holy Spirit parallels the high priestly work of intercession by the Lord Jesus, our Great High Priest, on behalf of believers. No words are necessary because the Father understands and agrees with what the Spirit thinks.

We are praying to God the Father, in the power and knowledge of the Spirit, and in the name of Jesus. They are omnipotent, omniscient, and omnipresent. They know our thoughts and our prayers before we even utter them. But they are there in unison to accomplish God's will. Prayer helps us get our will in line with God's will.

The message in John 15:1-12 is all about the relationship we must have to be heard in our prayers. The Father needs to see we are abiding in Christ so that when our prayers come up in the power of the Spirit through the Son to the Father, they are bathed in righteousness because the Spirit and the Son will not ask for anything unrighteous before the Father. Jesus and the Spirit are, so to speak, our righteous filters. Jesus speaks of this abiding relationship and its results:

> *"If you abide in me, and my words abide in you, ask whatever you wish, and it will be done for you. By this my Father is glorified, that you bear much fruit and so prove to be my disciples"* (John 15:7,8).

This message is the key to our entire prayer life: *Abiding in Christ*. So, when we have that deep, abiding relationship with the Son, we also have that same relationship with the Father. And we will not ask for anything that is not in line with His will. But, if we do, the Spirit will utter groanings for us that align with the will of the Father. We may not get the answer we want when we want it, but we will one day receive the correct answer, all according to the will of the Father.

So, pray to the Father, in the power of the Holy Spirit, and in the name of Jesus. Amen and amen!

Testimony by John Roper
Senior Vice President of CBRE, Dallas, Texas

Prayer is such an incredible gift from the LORD because it provides us with the most precious access, communion, and two-way communication with our Almighty, Holy KING. It cost the LORD so much to provide believers with the gracious gift of this access to Himself through the Perfect, Atoning Sacrifice of His Son, JESUS, Who suffered & died on the cross as our Risen SAVIOR.

Oswald Chambers describes prayer, "We look upon prayer simply as a means of getting things for ourselves, but the Biblical purpose of prayer is that we may get to know God Himself." As I continue to walk with my LORD and SAVIOR, I am learning that prayer is as much about being quiet, centering on Him, soaking up His Presence, and listening for the Spirit's voice. For much of my life, my prayers were a monologue and I've realized that the most important part is hearing from my Master. JESUS said, "My sheep hear my voice; I know them and they follow Me" (John 10:27).

I wanted to share a testimony that God used to greatly encourage me in my faith in prayer. One evening in 2016, I was attending an open-air house church in Latin America. As we were nearing the end of a special time of worship and teaching, the female pastor came over to me and my interpreter to ask if I would pray for the specific healing of some of the women at the front. My interpreter translated that I needed to pray for His healing from a seated position. If I stood up and prayed, it might be viewed by potential communists in attendance as a visiting pastor who was preaching and teaching without a Visa. I prayed with my right hand outstretched toward the women up front.

Praying in faith for their healing, I referenced the story from Luke 8:43-48, in which the woman who was bleeding for twelve years desperately reached out in faith to touch the hem of JESUS' robe, and she was healed instantly by our SAVIOR. I broke down crying as I prayed, "LORD JESUS, I'm reaching out to touch the hem of Your robe for these women who need Your Healing! Touch them and bring them Your gracious gift of healing for the Glory of Your Name." In that moment, I sensed the Almighty passing by and responding with His Love, Grace, and Compassion. I experienced the Power and Majesty of His Presence.

As I closed my prayer in JESUS' Almighty and Most Powerful Name, I was deeply grateful for how the LORD had responded to my prayer. I didn't know what He had done regarding the specific healing requests, but I was most grateful to experience Him and His Greatness.

The next morning, the pastor came up to me and said with a crack in her voice, "I didn't mention my prayer request, but I needed healing." She continued sobbing, "I need a cane to walk long distances to see my congregation. While you were praying, my right thigh started to heat up and I cried out Hallelujah because I knew the LORD was healing me. God is so Good, Gracious, and Kind. I don't need my cane anymore."

Chapter 5
When do you pray?

I have my opinion, but I'll let God's word speak directly to the question of when to pray. First, it is essential to remember that prayer must be a top priority for all Christians. Many of us make the mistake of putting it second or third, often to work and family obligations. I once read somewhere that *"instead of making prayer fundamental, we make it supplemental."* Big mistake! That plays out when we make decisions and ask God to bless them as an afterthought.

In his letter to Timothy, Paul sheds light on where to pray:

"I desire then that in every place the men should pray" (I Tim. 2:8a).

The scripture unpacks the meaning of *"every place,"* which should be interpreted as *"any place"* for the believer:

"And on the Sabbath day we went outside the gate to the riverside, where we supposed there was a place of prayer" (Acts 16:13a).

"In these days he (Jesus) went out to the mountain to pray, and all night he continued in prayer to God" (Luke 6:12).

"And rising very early in the morning, while it was still dark, he [Jesus] departed and went out to a desolate place, and there he prayed" (Mark 1:35).

And when Paul writes to the Thessalonians, he says the following about when to pray:

"Rejoice always, pray without ceasing, give thanks in all circumstances; for this is the will of God in Christ Jesus for you" (I Thess. 5:16,17).

Do you notice the imperatives? Always, without ceasing, in all circumstances. This one passage covers the "when"—but wait, there is more:

> *"Praying at all times in the Spirit, with all prayer and supplication. To that end, keep alert with all perseverance, making supplication for all the saints"* (Eph. 6:18).

> *"Continue steadfastly in prayer, being watchful in it with thanksgiving"* (Col. 4:2).

Again, pay attention to the language used: *praying at all times, in the Spirit, with supplication* (i.e., humbly), *steadfastly*. But also note the instructions to *keep alert* and *be watchful with thanksgiving*. Those aspects of praying are easy to gloss over, but they make the difference between truly communicating with God and waiting for His guidance and simply speaking your prayer in a rush or by rote.

As in Old Testament times, you may feel compelled to pray when you're outnumbered, and it's just you and the Lord vs. (seemingly) everyone else. You might need a mighty miracle! Consider Elijah, who never prayed for small things. He was alone amid all the prophets of Baal, plus probably many others. It was a time for the Israelites to decide who they would worship. For Elijah, it was time to pray and watch God!

> *"And at the time of the offering of the oblation, Elijah the prophet came near and said, 'O Lord, God of Abraham, Isaac, and Israel, let it be known this day that you are God in Israel, and that I am your servant, and that I have done all these things at your word. Answer me, O Lord, answer me, that this people may know that you, O Lord, are God, and that you have turned their hearts back'"* (I Kings 18:36,37).

At that moment, fire fell from heaven and burned up the offering, and the people fell on their faces and worshiped. This passage shows me that you never know what God might do when you pray in the presence of others.

Many years ago, I was trying to figure out how to live victoriously, one day at a time. God led me to my life verses, which, among other things, speak of when to pray:

> *"But seek first the kingdom of God and his righteousness, and all these things will be added to you. Therefore do not be anxious about*

tomorrow, for tomorrow will be anxious for itself. Sufficient for the day is its own trouble" (Mt. 6:33,34).

This Scripture has reminded me that I must seek Him and His righteousness early each day through His word and prayer. And that I should not worry about tomorrow because it still belongs to Him and not me.

In other passages, we are encouraged to give the first fruits of our labor to God. That, to me, means we should give the "first fruits" of our lives every morning to our relationship with God through the word and prayer.

On this matter I will quote my prayer mentor, the late E. M. Bounds:

"I feel it is far better to begin with God, to see His face first, to get my soul near Him before it is near another. In general, it is best to have at least one hour alone with God before engaging in anything else."

"If God is not first in our thoughts and efforts in the morning, he will be in the last place the remainder of the day."

"True prayers are born of present trials and present needs. Bread for today is bread enough. Bread given for today is the strongest sort of pledge that there will be bread tomorrow. Victory today is the assurance of victory tomorrow. Our prayers need to be focused upon the present. We must trust God today, and leave tomorrow entirely with him. The present is ours; the future belongs to God. Prayer is the task and duty of each recurring day – daily prayer for daily needs."

"The men who have done the most for God in this world have been early on their knees. He who fritters away the early morning, it's opportunity and freshness, in other pursuits than seeking God will make poor headway seeking Him the rest of the day."

The model prayer given to us by Jesus reinforces the wisdom of starting each day in prayer:

"Our Father in heaven, hallowed be your name. Your kingdom come, your will be done on earth, as it is in heaven. <u>Give us this day our daily bread</u>…" (Mt. 6:9-13).

E. M. Bounds offers a helpful interpretation of this familiar passage:

> *"When we pray, 'Give us this day our daily bread,' we are, in a measure, shutting tomorrow out of our prayer. We do not live in tomorrow but in today. We do not seek tomorrow's grace or tomorrow's bread. They thrive best, and get most out of life, who live in the living present. They pray best who pray for today's needs, not for our tomorrow's, which may render our prayers unnecessary and redundant by not existing at all!"*

While public and corporate prayer are appropriate, Jesus encourages us to get alone, a place of quietness, to hear God's voice. He wants us to draw near to Him, and to experience more of Him. Today, we call this our *"quiet time."* And we need much of the time to be still and listen for His voice. Read Matthew's instruction below:

> *"And when you pray, you must not be like the hypocrites. For they love to stand and pray in the synagogues and at the street corners, that they may be seen by others. Truly, I say to you, they have received their reward. But when you pray, go into your room and shut the door and pray to your Father who is in secret. And your Father who sees in secret will reward you"* (Mt. 6:5,6).

The Psalmist also suggests praying not only during our morning routine but also while still awake in our beds at night:

> *"When I remember You on my bed, I meditate on You in the night watches"* (Psa. 63:6 NKJV).

So, when to pray? When you feel compelled by the Spirit to pray anywhere, anytime, for anyone, and about anything. And to do it right then and there.

Throughout my life, I have found that whenever someone shares a concern about themselves or someone else, I ask for the privilege of praying for that situation at that very moment. I have never been rejected.

Recently, while changing in the men's locker room after my daily workout, one

CHAPTER 5 - WHEN DO YOU PRAY?

of my new friends at the gym shared a severe concern about his wife's health and what she was going through. I asked that we pray for her right then. He agreed. I prayed, and he said, "Amen" at the end. Then, he said, *"Bill, I've prayed a lot of times but never naked."* (He had just finished showering.) As I said, anywhere, anytime, and for anything! You want God to be glorified. So, pray!

The fact is, there is never a wrong time to pray. Now that we've settled the "when" (and where) let's move on to…what do we pray for?

Testimony by David Rodriguez
ENGAGE Monthly Prayer Ministry Coordinator for Dallas Real Estate Ministries (DREM), Dallas, Texas

Learning to pray began in 1980, the year I became a Christian and a believer in Jesus Christ, at the age of 29.

Prior to becoming a believer, I had prayed before, having grown up in another religious faith until I was 19…and before becoming agnostic for the next 10 years. So, in my youth and teens, it was just repeating words, somewhat heartfelt, but I was not sure if my prayers were really worthy of being heard.

As a new believer, I still carried that early thinking—if I prayed and then messed up later in the day, my prayers were not worthy of being heard by God.

If you are reading this account and fall into the same category and line of thinking in your present stage of Christian life, I am sharing how prayer can grow your understanding of our Savior and of His unconditional love for us that allows us daily—hourly—to come to Him with our burdens and cares, and to also pray for others and their needs. And in the process, we can experience a constant growth and intimate relationship in our faith, trust, and obedience to our Lord. We can also find forgiveness and grace from Him that leads to a better understanding of how much our Lord loves us.

As a new believer in Christ, I was always in awe of how some mature Christians prayed as if it was a natural conversation—some just praising Him over and over. My thinking was that you had to be 100 percent sin-free and guilt-free to speak/pray/praise Him that way, as I struggled to know what to say and how to say it with ease and comfort.

This went on for the first 15 years of my Christian life. When I was 45 years old, an elder of the church I was attending asked me if I liked to pray. Of course, I said yes. Then he asked me a very life-changing question: Had I ever prayed for an hour and/or would I like to learn to pray for an hour? My immediate thought was, "You've got to be kidding…get a life!!" But I answered yes so as not to embarrass myself or feel guilty by saying no.

So, I asked what was involved (while thinking, what have I gotten myself into?). Expecting a book or pamphlet, I was handed a single one-page sheet. I was astonished at how simple the instructions were.

1. Give thanks to HIM first...SPEND AS MUCH TIME ON THIS FIRST...for who God is...what He has done for me... and that He loves us 24/7.

2. Confess before you pray...do not hide from him...run to HIM... He loves that...it is a healthy fear of God!!

3. Forgive people.

4. Pray for others and their needs.

5. Then pray for your needs.

6. End in praise for all HE will do in His timing...not your timing.

I could not believe that I had been in prayer for over an hour. I was humbled, overjoyed, and amazed that I could do it!

So, here is what I have learned in maturing in prayer these many years later at the age of 72...still using these 6 simple steps.

Prayer is simply talking to God. God wants us to communicate with him, and this is made possible by Jesus Christ's death on the cross for us.

Prayer can be done anywhere...at any time...at any place. No electricity is required...no lights...nothing.

For many, prayer is a learned behavior; learn to schedule time so it becomes a habit.

Start with five-second prayers or praises. God will take these all day long. "Thank you Lord...I love you ABBA, ABBA, ABBA Father... I confess to you..."

Find a quiet spot, just for a few minutes (or five seconds)…in your parked car…in the closet…in your office…in your backyard…wherever. Just close your eyes and shut out the world and thank God for how much He loves you—just pure thanks to him.

It's what I have been doing since learning to pray for an hour (or five seconds), and I still keep it simple…all day long. Prayer has changed my perspective on how much God loves me, no matter the situation or circumstances. He loves me all day long and I have grown to share that love for me with others…and to pray for their needs!!

Dallas Real Estate Ministries PRAYER MINISTRY

The "ENGAGE" Prayer Ministry was a turning point in my Christian growth at age 57 in terms of investing in others and their needs. I evolved from praying once a month over prayer request cards submitted by individuals in the community, to the Holy Spirit prompting me to pray more often for those people each month and to stay in contact with them.

This was now an additional time commitment, but I felt HIS JOY when doing it…and eventually, it became a natural part of my prayer life. It was then that I realized that God was using me to glorify HIM in letting people with prayer needs know I and others were praying for them.

I take no credit for this…I just finally let HIM take control of my actions and the joy that followed from HIM.

Testimony by Annie D'Spain
Pediatric Nurse, Washington Regional Hospital, Fayetteville, Arkansas

As I reflect on my prayer journey, I marvel at the freedom we have been given through prayer. Prayer has looked differently in each season of my life, which has furthered my faith in believing that "The LORD is near to all who call on him, to all who call on Him in truth" (Psa. 145:18). At the beginning of my personal walk with the Lord, I remember hearing many older women pray and thinking, "Wow, I wish I could pray like that someday," while at the same time battling with the lie from the enemy that I would never have the depth of those women's faith to be able to do so. I recall battling these thoughts one day when I came across Hebrews 4:16, which says, "Let us then with confidence draw near to the throne of grace, that we may receive mercy and find grace to help in time of need." While reading that, I recognized that I, too, no matter how young or old my faith is, can come to Him with confidence in prayer.

The summer before my senior year of college, I spent a month on a church mission in Uganda, and while there, I found the incredible value of writing my prayers down in a journal. I often struggled with being distracted by my thoughts and was often more prone to pray lofty words aloud. But when I wrote them down, I didn't write everything that came to mind. I took time to sit, think, and reflect before I wrote. I found that the time I spent pondering before praying led me to pray more intentionally and boldly.

One season of my life in which prayer looked differently than previously was when I began my nursing career on the night shift. Because of this, most of the hours I was awake, my husband, family, and friends were asleep, but the Lord was not, and He became a constant companion to me in the night.

At the same time, as my husband and I entered marriage, we considered how to merge our individual prayer lives with one another. While we both felt that praying together before bed each night would be valuable, it was easy to find reasons not to think that could be possible for us due to my husband studying to be a doctor and my being at the hospital at night. But after many situations where it became evident to us the fruit of praying with one another consistently, and continuing to have the stirring of the Spirit on us that this would be of great value, we determined to be faithful to it. While each night looks different, whether over the phone or in person, it has been a unifying pursuit for us both, and we continue to see the blessings from it.

As I recently entered motherhood, I remember in the beginning stages of having a newborn, thinking to myself, "I don't know how I'll ever have the time I used to have to sit and journal my prayers each morning." While that season may come again one day, I sought to find the new rhythm that He was calling me to in this season. My prayers are often shorter during the day as my now toddler is as curious as ever. However, I now feel that "praying without ceasing," which I once thought impossible, is more attainable as we invite Him into our thoughts and lives throughout the day.

With each new season comes new ways for us to call upon Him, and I am abundantly grateful for the ways the Lord meets us where we are and eagerly awaits us to draw near to Him at the throne of grace.

Chapter 6
What do you pray for?

Again, the short answer is...*anything and everything!* Scripture is very clear on this. Meditate on what the Spirit writes through Paul to the Corinthian church, which I have underlined for emphasis.

"Rejoice in the Lord always; again I will say rejoice. Let your reasonableness be known to everyone. The Lord is at hand; do not be anxious about <u>anything</u>, but in <u>everything</u> by <u>prayer and supplication with thanksgiving</u> let your requests be made known to God. And the <u>peace of God</u>, which surpasses all understanding, <u>will guard</u> your hearts and your minds in Christ Jesus" (Phil. 4:6,7).

This is a recipe for prayerful living. We live in a world that is broken. Anxiety impacts everyone. We encounter so many people along the way. How can we rejoice with everything that's going on in the world, our family, our own life, and our heart? The Spirit gives us the answer. We are not to worry about anything; instead, we need to lay everything before the Lord through prayer and supplication, with thanksgiving. Then, God promises to grant us the peace that surpasses all understanding. And by doing so, we can rejoice and be victorious in our lives and with everyone we meet.

God is involved in every minute detail of our lives. We are His, and He is ours. And He wants us to succeed and bring glory to His name. At the same time, He brings us peace that does not exist in the world. And I don't have to tell you that Satan, while not omnipresent, omniscient, or omnipotent, is powerful, and he is interested in destroying your peace by whatever means possible. This is a critical reason to pray about everything and leave nothing to chance.

John writes in I John 4:4 that as children of God (paraphrased), *"we have overcome the world, and He (Jesus) who is in us is greater than he (Satan) who is in the world."* Prayer allows you to realize this truth—and gain victory!

We see that everything needs to be brought before the Lord in prayer. Doing so removes our self-dependence and places it in the hands of the One who has already been victorious through the cross, the empty tomb, and the ascension. Know that Jesus is our High Priest seated at the right hand of the Father, Creator, Redeemer, and Sustainer, and He, Jesus, is interceding for you and me every single moment.

Prayer is all about change. Ever since the fall of Adam and Eve, we have experienced sin of every nature in us and in the world. Prayer is an agent of change. As R. C. Sproul says, *"What prayer most often changes is the wickedness and the hardness of our own hearts."*

As I mentioned earlier in the book, I was in Washington, D.C., several years ago praying for our country before a national election with others. A local pastor delivered a message about the power of prayer. Afterward, he looked straight at me and said, *"Bill, you do know that God runs His universe, His kingdom, through the prayers of His people?"*

That profound thought has impacted my prayer life ever since. God has given His saints, born-again believers here on Earth, the privilege, responsibility, and authority to bring about His kingdom purposes and usher in Jesus' return. How? Through obedient, believing prayer.

No prayer is too small or too large. He hears them all. And He will eventually answer every prayer, even on the day of judgment, if His will is to take that long. Prayer involves praise, so we must enter into our prayer time—no matter where, no matter when—with an attitude of praise and thanksgiving.

You may be dealing with the sin in your life and the need for forgiveness and repentance. You may be praying for your family, marriage, children, parents, whoever. You can intercede on behalf of people in your inner circle and extended neighborhood as well as the country and worldwide. We are told to pray for our leaders, whether we agree or disagree politically. We are to lift up the sick for healing and restoration and are encouraged to call the elders together to pray over them. We should extend prayers for the salvation of family, friends, and even enemies.

Tragic events prophesied in the Bible are being fulfilled in our lifetime: wars, earthquakes and other natural disasters, pestilences, diseases, crimes of every nature, family dysfunction, abortion, sexual and gender confusion, and many more. None of these are good. Knowing God hears us, we are encouraged to pray and believe in the meaning of these situations and circumstances. We are invoking His power, love, and wisdom when we pray. It's not about us or our power but about Him and His power. Prayer executes this for us and for others.

Be specific with God. This way, when He answers the prayer in His own time and in His own way, you will know and be encouraged that He heard you and acted on your prayer.

> *"Then he said to me, 'Fear not, Daniel, for from the first day that you set your heart to understand and humbled yourself before your God, your words have been heard, and I have come because of your words. The prince of the kingdom of Persia withstood me twenty-one days, but Michael, one of the chief princes, came to help me, for I was left there with the kings of Persia, and came to make you understand what is to happen to your people in the latter days. For the vision is for days yet to come'"* (Dan.10:12-14).

Keeping a prayer journal can also be encouraging, as you can record answered prayers and use them to deepen your faith in times of need. Be patient: Some answers come quickly, and others beyond your lifetime. But they all count, and they are all heard. We can say this about others in our lives, but we can never say this about God: *"I don't know why I tell you anything because you never listen to me."*

Testimony by Robyn Bush
Widowed Mom of Three

Praying in "The Wait"

Life is filled with an abundance of *waiting*. Seldom are we content with our lives, our circumstances and relationships, just as they are, and we often spend plenty of prayer time talking to God about it. God's word says much about our "waiting," for in our "wait," God is doing something far greater than we can imagine, and prayer helps us discover a treasure worthy of the wait.

> Psalm 27:14 says,
> "Wait for the LORD: be strong, and let your heart take courage;
> wait for the LORD!"

Waiting also provides fertile ground for worry and anxiety to grow. When our circumstances and relationships aren't met instantly, our gaze can become transfixed upon them and lead us into a host of lies. It is easy to lose heart and hope quickly when our prayers seemingly go unanswered. We are often quick to doubt God's character or ability, believing He doesn't hear, care, or have our best interests at heart.

But if we take God at His word and press into the reality that He is good and does good, God changes us, and purifies us in the wait! My own life has held many challenging seasons of waiting. Seasons marked by joyful expectation and seasons of wait that were painfully marked by fear, brokenness, and loss. In those seasons of waiting, prayer has become a transformative gift that brings me into the presence of the One true constant. For His presence and nature is unchanging, compassionate, and steady in the midst of the wait. He anchors me, us, into His dynamic presence and upon a firm foundation.

Several years ago, I sat in an Intensive Care Unit at the bedside of my husband. He had unexpectedly suffered a massive stroke, and our family was in a painful season of waiting as to whether he would survive. My fears were palpable, and tears came often as I sat holding his hand. My raw heart was drawn into prayer over and over again in that wait. With few words, I poured out my heart to the One I knew…knew all, and could do all. In those prayers, those intimate confessions intermingled with faith, God was preparing my heart for what lay ahead. He tenderly stripped away the false comforts my heart was holding onto and drew me into His arms, the strong arms of a Shepherd who held my heart so tenderly as the wait came to an end.

It wasn't the outcome my heart had desired, but God had prepared me in the wait, teaching me to take courage and trust His heart. This is why prayer is a transformative gift, particularly in the wait, for in the secret prayer chamber of our hearts, our gaze has the opportunity to be rightly affixed to the One who IS truly in control. The One who sees, knows, and rules over all, and who is loving, conforming us into the image of His Son. This is the treasure to be found in the prayerful waiting—more of His intimate presence.

VICTORY THROUGH PRAYER!

Chapter 7
The Impact of Prayer

I thought I would begin this chapter with helpful prompts: What noticeable results have you experienced in your prayer life? Were you surprised, pleased, joyful, disappointed, resigned, or otherwise? Do you remember praying in faith, believing God would hear and answer your prayers? Was the prayer about you or your family, friends, co-workers, or church? Or maybe you lifted a missionary or the nation in prayer?

Also, what distinct answers have you received in response to what you prayed for? Did the answers encourage you in your prayer life? How did they impact your view of God? Were the answers what you expressly asked for? Or did God reveal a different plan? What about the timing? Was it suitable for you or only for God?

Lastly, are there prayers you've been praying for a long time and have heard or seen no action on God's part? Does that impact your trust in God's sovereignty? Do you genuinely believe He wants the best for you and those you pray for? These are fundamental questions that we all face in one way or another as we move through our life. Prayer is so personal, and we want everything we desire to be accomplished. Do you agree?

As we address these and so many more questions about prayer and God, we must realize that the most significant impact of prayer is on us. Why do I say that? Because just like Adam and Eve, we sinners want what we want, and we want it now. We have a tough time waiting. God, however, is in the business of sanctifying His sons and daughters for His glory. Prayer redirects our reliance on our abilities and strengths to patiently putting everything into the hands of the Almighty God, who created the heavens and the Earth and holds everything together. We must believe He is more than capable of answering our prayers with the appropriate results and the desirable impact on His people.

Throughout our lives, we believers will offer thousands of prayers, or at least we should. The prayers are intercessory, praise, confession, repentance, and supplication. No prayer is too small or too large for God to handle. We should approach prayer, desiring results that align with God's word and His plan for His kingdom, now and for eternity—and not what we believe to be the "right" answer.

Think of it this way: A father, a godly father, wants the very best for his family, his children, and the next generations. He will not knowingly allow something that would bring harm to them. But sometimes, a father's (and a mother's) prayers are for difficult things to bring about changes and blessings in our families. Our heavenly Father knows our every need and the needs of all those we are praying for, and He will answer them and bring the results and impact in keeping with His righteousness, holiness, and plan for eternity. The impacts and results will be within you and within the people or circumstances for which you are praying.

One of the most significant prayers ever uttered was by Jesus himself the day before His crucifixion, which He knew was to happen. He went to be alone in the Garden of Gethsemane, leaving three of His disciples behind. There, Jesus asked God the Father if there was any other way that the salvation of humankind could be accomplished, nevertheless saying that only the Father's will be done. Even in the face of death, Jesus wanted the results God the Father wanted. They had planned this. But the Son of Man knew the pain and separation He would endure as a human for the sake of you and me. The results are evident, and the impact is eternal. I believe Jesus was prepared to subject His will to His Father's to please Him. Are you willing to pray this way?

There are no boundaries on what you can pray for and about. As discussed elsewhere, Jesus clearly said that if you abide in Him and He abides in you, whatever you ask will be given to you. Don't you see that God, who gave His only Son to die on the cross and chose you to bear fruit for His kingdom, will also move heaven and Earth to provide the results and the impact you are praying for?

And those prayers are limitless. God hears prayers from billions of believers daily across the world. Yours are as important as all the rest. The Lord does not take the attitude, *"I'll get back to you later."* Everything is present with him. Your prayers are before Him as a sweet aroma, an incense that is pleasing to him. He desires to answer your prayers in His time and in a way that glorifies Him.

CHAPTER 7 - THE IMPACT OF PRAYER

But the prayers must be in accordance with His word, which reflects His will.

Over the 50 years I have spent teaching in prisons virtually every week, I observed the power of prayer in many circumstances in these inmates' lives. Most, if not all, have spent years, even decades, without any contact with their children. This is one of the most depressing aspects of their lives. They have genuine regret and sadness. I/we have encouraged men to continue communicating with their families even if they don't respond. But the most impactful thing I have seen is when we sit with these men and pray specifically, sometimes weekly, for the relationships to be restored. I can honestly say that I have seen numerous miracles with children, clearly out of the blue, communicating with their father in some manner. And many of the relationships become restored, even before the men are released.

Now I would like to share a personal story that demonstrates how gracious our Lord is. In 2009, I was retiring from a career in the real estate industry. I had numerous interests in property investments, which I had worked on when I was with Jim Williams at LandPlan. As happens over a lifetime, the economy, at least the part relating to real estate, plummeted. My wife Joanne and I still had a mortgage on our home, and I had run out of funds to keep these investments going. Simply put, I was between the proverbial rock and a hard place. As a husband, I was ashamed and anxious.

Knowing this was a highly uncertain time, I did what I always do when there's no apparent answer. I fell on my face in prayer, putting my business interests, the debt on our house, and our future into God's hands. I told God I wouldn't do anything but trust Him. I met with Jim, and we carved out a reasonable deal for him to buy out most of my interests in the coming year. One of them was a hospital in Frisco that we had developed. I kept praying specifically for God to bring someone to buy that hospital before the end of the year and asked Joanne and a few friends to pray for that as well. I never called Jim over the next four months. I just kept falling on my face and trusting God. Joanne continued, rightly so, to ask me if I was going to meet with Jim since time was drawing near. In this instance, I did not want to have any knowledge or influence. I just wanted to see God at work firsthand and for Him to be glorified.

A little before Christmas, I got a call from Jim asking me to meet with him.

I figured it was about our agreement. We sat down together. He pushed two pieces of paper forward…and asked me, "Which of these do you want?" One was the agreement that he and I had already signed. The other was for the hospital sale that would happen before the end of the year. It was more than triple the amount that was in our agreement. Jim could have closed on the executed contract, but as a believer and a dear friend, he chose to bless us with this hospital sale.

There is much more to this story, but the bottom line is that we paid off the mortgage on our home and every other debt we owed. Within a few months, I was challenged by the Lord to write *From Faith to Faith*, and out of that grew a fatherhood discipleship ministry called *Abiding* Fathers (more on this below). Along the way, God clearly whispered in my ear, "Is there any question as to who is leading your life?" My answer was, and is, a resounding NO!!!

Looking back on this, I see God's plan to create that global ministry through me. He placed Joanne and me in a position to accomplish this with His financial support.

Prayer, fervent prayer, yields results and impacts God's kingdom. The overriding fruit has been a peace that surpasses all understanding in Christ Jesus. What a privilege to pray to the God of the universe. Pray, keep on praying, always believing with thanksgiving.

P.S. Two very significant events in my life, ministry-wise, came about in the following ways. One morning in 1986, I was awakened around 3 a.m. I was aware that there was something different about the moment. I sensed that I needed to get on my knees and listen. Among many other things, what I heard numerous times over three hours was this. *"I want to build a spiritual house in the real estate community of Dallas Texas."*

Today, as a result of this, God is still building a spiritual house in Dallas in accordance with I Peter 2.4,5. *"As you come to him, a living stone rejected by men but in the sight of God chosen and precious, you yourselves like living stones are being built up as a spiritual house, to be a holy priesthood, to offer spiritual sacrifices acceptable to God through Jesus Christ."* The ministry is Dallas Real Estate Ministries (drem.org).

The other is the origin of *Abiding* Fathers (abidingfathers.org). Thirty years into teaching the Bible each week in the Seagoville Federal Correctional Institution, Hutchins State Jail, and Union Gospel Mission, I was in my morning quiet time. The Godhead laid on my heart that the number one issue in America today was the absentee father, having seen the devastating results firsthand with these incarcerated and homeless men. The overwhelming majority of them had an absentee father in their life. I was in my regular Bible reading and prayer when I sensed God's still, small voice. I asked God if it was Him. Then, in my mind's eye, I saw the words *From Faith to Faith*. Almost immediately, this message was clearly present—from fathers absent in the home to fathers abiding in the home. John 15:1-12 became the foundational verses for the creation of *Abiding* Fathers.

These testimonies speak to the incredible value of sometimes just listening while being in prayer and His word for Him to speak to you in whatever way He chooses. I know you have your stories. I would love to hear them (send me an email: bill@life-today.org).

Testimony by Annie Roberson
Community Liaison, Disciple City Church, Dallas, Texas

In my early stage of salvation, I was a member of a local church that was inspirational in leading me to salvation. As I began to grow and witness for the Lord—including weekly Bible studies, memorizing Scripture, and attending church on a regular basis (not sporadically as I normally did)—I encountered some problems within the church, which blocked my spiritual growth. So what was I supposed to do? How do you handle this problem biblically?

This experience turned my heart to seeking the Lord in prayer. How often are we told to take our burdens to the Lord and leave them there? You ask God for His wisdom according to James 1:5, which says, "But if any of you lacks wisdom, let him ask of God, who gives to all men generously and without reproach, and it will be given to him."

I had a tough decision to make. Do I stay here and sit, soak, and sour, or do I move on with my two very young daughters? (They were 3 years and 11 months old; my third had not yet been born.) It was a tough decision, but through prayer, I decided to move on.

In the process of doing that, I was labeled as a "troublemaker" to the next church I had planned to join. Of course, I tried to defend myself, but being a "baby" Christian with no status against that kind of accusation was troubling. I was told by the receiving pastor not to attend his church for a month because of the situation. This angered me, thinking, "I don't have to take this; I can go anywhere I want to go and certainly not there either."

However, my Christian friend and co-worker told me to do what they asked me to do. Throughout the entire process, anger and all, I asked the Lord to "vindicate me." When the word came into my Spirit, I didn't even know what it meant. However, at the end of a month of visiting other churches, I was allowed to join the receiving church. I continued to grow there in my spiritual journey with the Lord and to trust in Him completely through prayer, faith, and obedience to the "Word." I was even exalted to serve there in an executive position. I know that prayer works! I depend on it.

"The prayers of the righteous availeth much" (James 5:16). Don't stop praying! Your life depends on it. Always know that the Lord works on your behalf.

VICTORY THROUGH PRAYER!

Chapter 8
The Family Prayer

As mentioned in the introduction, I was inspired two decades ago by Dr. John Richard—the father of Ramesh Richard, founder and CEO of RREACH—who had created a daily prayer for his family. I began to pray over various scriptures and focus on what I wanted to see God do daily and for the rest of their lives. Namely, I desired that their existence here on Earth would be filled with purpose and that God would fulfill that purpose.

Ramesh granted permission to share his father's daily family prayer, which follows:

"O Blessed Trinity, may Your benediction resting upon me and my wife be passed on to our children, our children's children, and the generations to come! May their lives be as a sweet-smelling savor! May they exude the fragrance of the Lord Jesus Christ! May their outward lives, which men see, bring much credit to our Master's name!

May they all be filled with all the fullness of God! May they be complete in Christ! May rivers of living water flow from their innermost being! May they irradiate the beauty, the mind, and the character of Christ! May they reflect like mirrors the glory and the grace of the Lord Jesus Christ! May they all be full-time Christians and some among them even full-time Christian workers! May they be reconcilers, reconciling people with God, people with people, repairers of the breaches, bridge-builders! May they scatter sunshine wherever they go; may they distill the dews of peace wherever they go! May none of them be lost unto perdition!"

Amen and amen! May this excellent example inspire you to create your own family prayer with God and the Bible as your guide.

As recorded in John 17, Jesus prayed an earthly prayer for the family of God that is still pertinent and alive today. I thought how great it would be if my prayer would endure throughout many generations of my earthly family. Of course, I am not the Son of God, so the goal is for the Holy Spirit to work in and through these prayers. I was admittedly concerned that repeating the same prayer day in and day out would become rote and devoid of meaning, but that soon subsided.

In addition to this daily family prayer, I pray for each individual specifically—my wife, daughters, grandchildren, and great-grandchildren. I pray for them by name and address any issues I know they are facing. I also pray they will realize what God wants to accomplish in their walk with the Lord here on Earth. This simple act brings me great peace, knowing I have lifted my loved ones up to His will.

Fathers, I encourage you to create one for your family prayerfully. God has given you the authority to be the priest of your family. This is not to discount the prayers of a mother. They accomplish much.

Here, then, is my "Priestly Prayer:"

> *"Dear gracious heavenly Father, thank you for covering my family with your banner of love.*
>
> *Thank you for anointing my family with the atoning blood of Jesus, your only begotten Son, our only Savior.*
>
> *Thank you for cleansing my family from all unrighteousness through the shed blood of Jesus, our propitiation, our substitute, our atonement, our all-in-all.*
>
> *Thank you for filling and sealing my family with your promised Holy Spirit, doing in my family what you want to do through them, and leading my family in paths of righteousness for your name's sake.*
>
> *Thank you for surrounding my family with your holy angels, providing a hedge of protection for my family, and keeping my family from harm's way.*
>
> *Thank you for clothing my family in your full armor: the belt of truth, the breastplate of righteousness, feet shod with the gospel of peace, the*

> *shield of faith, the helmet of salvation, and the sword of the Spirit, which is the word of God.*
>
> *Thank you for providing prayer, that my family might be prayerful, watchful, alert, steadfast, immovable, always abounding in the work of the Lord, knowing that this work is not in vain in the Lord.*
>
> *Thank you for preserving my family from all evil, preserving their soul, preserving their going out and their coming in from this time forth and even forevermore.*
>
> *Thank you for uniting our family in Christ, in Christ alone, and doing great and mighty things in and through us today, and all the days of our lives.*
>
> *In the perfect name of Jesus, all to your glory, Heavenly Father. Amen."*

You might feel that beginning each petition with "thank you" is a little redundant. But repeating these words puts my mind and heart in a mode of gratitude. Thanking Him in advance says that I believe He will hear my pleas. To me, it is an act of faith—praying and believing!

This approach to prayer is also based on the encouragement in Philippians 4:6,7 (NKJV; underlined for emphasis):

> *"Be anxious for nothing, but in everything by prayer and supplication, <u>with thanksgiving</u>, let your requests be made known to God, and the peace of God, which surpasses all understanding, shall guard your hearts and minds through Christ Jesus."*

There is victory through your priestly prayer for your family. Early and daily, I might add! As demonstrated in the testimony on the next page, you might not see the fruits of your prayers before you die, but trust God to answer them in His time and in His way.

Testimony by Dr. Jeffrey Parker
Pastor at the House of Prayer and Executive Director at Restoration Outreach Dallas (ROD)

I have come to understand the power of prayer, as I have witnessed my parents' prayers being answered even after their passing. Growing up in a small Methodist church in Shreveport, Louisiana, I was introduced to Christ at an early age. However, I never received proper guidance on how to live my life with Christ and ended up walking away from the church after finishing high school. Although I attended church for over 18 years, I never truly became a born-again believer in Christ as my parents' faith in Christ did not become mine.

After finishing college and before joining the military, I began studying Islam. I had been a Christian for 18 years, but Islam provided me with answers to social injustices that I witnessed daily. I remember questioning how our society could call itself Christian when it allowed such injustices to occur. I decided to embrace Islam and called my mother to inform her of my decision. Her response was simply, "Okay, Jeff," but I later found out that she went to God in prayer on my behalf. She must have reminded Him of the proverb that says, "Train up a child in the way he should go, and when he is old, he will not depart from it."

Prayer is not about getting what you want when you want it. Even when I didn't have the mindset to pray, someone else was praying for me. After I left the Armed Forces and took a job at United Parcel Service (UPS), the Lord sent a pastor dressed in browns to challenge me in a way I had never been challenged before.

I was then an over-the-road driver and experiencing a crisis of faith. I felt like God was going to take my life because I heard a voice saying, "Come back to me, or you will die." The rain made truck driving very challenging, and it seemed to heavily rain every day. One night, while driving, it rained so hard that I couldn't see the road, fearing that it was my last night on Earth. I was driving in and out of my lane when a voice over the CB radio asked who was in the truck.

It was Pastor Lynch. He answered my mother's prayers, though I was not saved in a church but in a truck. I gave my life to Christ, and Pastor Lynch became my mentor. I am now a pastor at the House of Prayer and have started fifty-eight churches. I also started three schools and serve as the Executive Director of Restoration Outreach Dallas/ROD Ministries, all because of the power of prayer!

VICTORY THROUGH PRAYER!

Chapter 9
Prayer Journaling

To me, prayer journaling is *remembrance*. I find it interesting that the Holy Spirit dictated through Moses the first five books of the Bible, the Pentateuch. Moses experienced some but not all of what was written. We see many occasions where men of God were either asked by the Lord or took their own initiative to erect memorials, most always with stones. Research shows 63 different occurrences of this in the Bible. One of the most significant is recorded in the book of Joshua.

> *"Then Joshua set up twelve stones in the midst of the Jordan, in the place where the feet of the priests who bore the ark of the covenant stood; and they are there to this day"* (Josh. 4:9).

It is referred to as the *"Twelve Stones of Remembrance."* Each stone represented one of the twelve tribes of Israel. God had held back the raging floodwaters of the Jordan so the priests could carry the ark across, and the people could walk across on dry ground, entering the Promised Land. Verse seven tells us that the stones were to be a memorial to the children of Israel forever. While the stones are a remembrance, the journal (book) of Joshua is as well.

The memorials were evidence, or a "sign," of what God had done for the nation. And, as stated, it was for the countless future generations. These generations need to sense their attachment to the past and know how faithful God is.

I have written many things over the years—family poems, devotionals, and now six books. I also journaled over the years, primarily in the Bible I was using at the time. It is easy to record something in the margins alongside a verse, jotting down what it meant to you, what God did or spoke through the words, or simply a relevant prayer request. The future generations reading your Bible will get a sense of your walk with the Lord. Unfortunately, one of my most significant Bibles was a Bill Glass version that was stolen while I was teaching the scripture at a Texas prison. Over 20 years, I recorded countless answered prayers in that Bible. It was heartbreaking to lose, though I trust that God used that Bible and my notes to claim the heart of the person who stole it.

My wife Joanne is an avid journaler, and has been for many years. She uses several forms of journals to record her observations, thoughts and insights. From time to time she goes back and reviews what she had written for various reasons. She has seen many answers to her previous prayers.

I want to share a story that is a significant act of love through journaling. A friend of mine, Holt Lunsford, shared that his father journaled in a separate Bible for each of his children, grandchildren, and great-grandchildren over one year after their birth, writing specifically about that person. He then gifted the Bibles to each child. At his recent funeral, each recipient walked forward and laid their Bible on the stage to honor him. Journaling takes many forms.

Different journals are available to meet various needs. Some guide you daily with verses or devotionals so that you may read and reflect. Others are filled with blank pages. A few years ago, my grandson, Luke, designed a journal for *Abiding* Fathers, the ministry God founded through me. On the blue faux-leather cover is the logo and the word ABIDE. It has been in high demand for various purposes. In 2022, my daughter, Evelyn, and I designed a 40-day devotional using a selection of my "*Life* Today" messages, allowing space to journal about the message for that day. These are but a few of the many journals from which to choose. And there's always the standard white or yellow notepads from school days. Whatever inspires you to put pen to paper.

Here are but a few scriptures that address *remembering*:

> *"Remember the days of old; consider the years of many generations; ask your father, and he will show you, your elders, and they will tell you"* (Deut. 32:7).

> *"Only take care, and keep your soul diligently, lest you forget the things that your eyes have seen, and lest they depart from your heart all the days of your life. Make them known to your children and your children's children"* (Deut. 4:9).

> *"Remember the former things of old; for I am God, and there is no other; I am God, and there is none like me"* (Isa. 46:9).

CHAPTER 9 - PRAYER JOURNALING

> *"I will remember the deeds of the Lord; yes, I will remember your wonders of old"* (Psa. 77:11).

> *"Remember the wondrous works that he has done, his miracles, and the judgments he uttered"* (Psa. 105:5).

> The Psalmist reminded Israel of their forgetfulness. *"Our fathers, when they were in Egypt, did not consider your wondrous works; they did not remember the abundance of your steadfast love, but rebelled by the sea, at the Red Sea"* (Psa. 106:7).

Journaling, or writing thoughts and prayers down during your quiet time, allows you to remember how faithful God has been to you. In times of dryness in your walk, it is good to look back and review much of what you have recorded.

Consider another story that is not biblical but helps make the point. People forget; all of us do. It's human nature. After World War II, General Dwight D. Eisenhower challenged people to take photos of the Holocaust in Germany. He reasoned that people would one day forget, even deny that it had ever happened. We are seeing that being played out today.

Even more so, Jesus was clear that He would send the Holy Spirit after He departed back to heaven so that the Spirit would bring remembrance back to the faithful of all that had happened, especially Jesus' death and resurrection.

> *"But the Helper, the Holy Spirit, whom the Father will send in my name, he will teach you all things and bring to your remembrance all that I have said to you"* (John 14.26).

So many things, some good and some not so good, help shape our lives. Journaling allows you to create a record of your concerns, your joys, your failures, and God's faithfulness. It will bring to your remembrance all God has said to or done for you. We forget—so write it down and journal in the way that best suits you.

Testimony by Rebecca Ellerman
Ministry Representative, Revive Our Hearts, Nationwide

"I have learned to see a need of everything God gives me, and want nothing that He denies me. Whether it be taken from or not given me, sooner or later God quiets me in Himself without it. I cast all my concerns on the Lord, and live securely on the care and wisdom of my Heavenly Father." Joseph Eliot *

I long for that to be true of me…One such provision God has given to help me live securely in the care and wisdom of my Father is through prayer and meditation *upon* God's Word. David's prayer recorded in Psalm 62 has been a great source of encouragement to remind me to seek and trust God alone, especially in times of uncertainty. And to ultimately find confident expectation by *faith* in God alone for His answer.

Stillness in His Presence is my greatest need.

> *"For God alone my soul waits in silence; from Him comes my salvation. He alone is my rock and my salvation, my fortress; I shall not be greatly shaken"* (vv.1,2).

This acknowledgment, uttered in agreement, becomes a formative "place" so that I am given a sacred "settlement" to steady my thoughts and become quiet before God.

Francois Fenelon said, "Silence promotes the presence of God…Silence humbles the mind, and gradually weans it from the world; it makes a kind of solitude in the heart."

Going forth in Psalm 62, a second echo resounds:

> *"For God alone, O my soul; wait in silence, for my hope is from Him"* (v.5).

Here I am led to counsel my soul to wait in silence for God. This indicates my willing consent (or participation) in the communion of prayer. His Word becomes both the counsel *of* my need as well as the desired outcome for my need. (The trajectory of my prayer is "God".) And using God's Word, I agree with God—and *place in remembrance* "my hope is from Him." Through His Spirit, I am made acutely aware of God, and my hope in Him is revived. It then becomes the fuel for this forward progression of turning every matter to Him.

Just as Psalm 62 illustrates, meditating on this interchange cultivates deeper stillness and quietness *with God*. His Word rises up and magnifies in my heart and mouth—and I am given eyes to see Him in a fuller way:

> *"He only is my rock and my salvation, my fortress; I shall not be shaken. On God rests my salvation and my glory; my mighty rock, my refuge is God"* (vv.6,7).

Notice these words: "my glory, my mighty rock, my refuge" is God. They become personal declarations. I believe them. God has given Himself to me in this communion of prayer. And that is where I'm quieted, resolute, and filled within so that what erupts is this crescendo of confident public declaration.

> *"Trust in Him at all times, O people; pour out your heart before Him; GOD IS a refuge for us"* (v.8).

It isn't necessarily in working out the situation, trial, or circumstance. With trust, He invites me to bring Him my cares and pour out my heart. And the result?

I am stilled and secured by His Presence.

He knows what is on my heart. He also gives me the freedom to intercede for others, with confidence in His lovingkindness. It is an extraordinary invitation. And as I place my cares upon Him, I trust Him with it. It's His now.

My hero of prayer is George Mueller. He dared to trust God by taking God at His Word. I frequently comb his biography concerning his way of faith and prayer:

> "Be encouraged, dear Christian reader, with fresh earnestness to give yourself to prayer, if you can only be sure that you ask for things which are for the glory of God."

Another saint of prayer, Charles Haddon Spurgeon, said:

> "It is a happy way of smoothing sorrow, when we can say, 'We will wait only upon God…come, cast your burden upon the Lord.' What seems to you a crushing burden, would be to Him but as the small dust of the balance. See! The Almighty bends his shoulders, and He says, 'Here, put thy troubles here." What! Wilt thou bear thyself what the everlasting shoulders are ready to carry?'"

So, in closing, will you join me in prayer?

"For God alone, O my soul; I wait in silence, for my hope is from You."

*Joseph Eliot (1638-1695) was the clergyman son of John Eliot (1604-1690), a Cambridge-educated Englishman who emigrated to America to evangelize the Indians of Massachusetts. Due to his tireless efforts on behalf of the Native Americans he loved, John Eliot was dubbed "The Apostle to the Indians." Joseph and his brother helped their father prepare *The Indian Grammar Begun* and translate the Bible into the Algonquin language.

Testimony by Sarah Peyton Ellerman

Ministry Leader for Female Youth Discipleship, Park Cities Presbyterian Church, Dallas, Texas

Prayer has come in many forms throughout my life. There are times when I pray sitting or on my knees, and times I pray on the go, whether on a walk or in the car. There are times when I pray prayers of gratitude, and there are times when I seek Him for clarity and discernment in making decisions. The older I get, the more I have learned that prayer is a conversation with my Heavenly Father and friend, which means sometimes I am the one talking, and sometimes I am listening. To be honest, this has not always been easy for me, and I often find myself distracted, but I'm thankful for His faithfulness and patience with me every step of the pilgrimage.

One of the habits I started from a young age was journaling my prayers in the morning. The act of writing down prayers of things I'm thankful for, things I'm wrestling with, and what the Lord is teaching me helps me to slow down and meditate on them. It also allows me to look back and see ways the Lord has answered.

In the Lord's sovereign and unique timing, a few years ago I picked up an old journal of mine from middle school and came across a prayer that I do not remember praying: "Dear God, I think you have put on my heart to be an encourager or, when I'm older, a small group leader." My eyes teared up as I read this (and not because of the grammar errors!) because ten years later, I found myself in a season of life where the Lord allowed me to walk alongside two middle school small groups. Those groups are now in high school, and I have had the privilege of leading them for four years.

What an awesome God we serve. He puts things on our hearts to pray for and answers them, even when we don't always remember asking for them. Without having written down that prayer, I wouldn't have remembered to thank Him or the opportunity to marvel at His sovereignty and kindness with this specific answer to prayer. This is just one example of answered prayers over the years of journaling that I have been able to see His answer and thank Him.

I will also acknowledge many prayers that either have not been answered (yet) or have been answered with a different result than I was seeking. I have spent hours of my life praying for specific requests and desires, praying for people to come to faith, and so on, and yet when faced with different outcomes or no visible answers, I choose to believe He hears me, sees me, and knows what is best for me. It is in these moments that I must remind myself of His character and heart, also recalling His faithfulness and consistency in being the same God yesterday, as He is today, as He will be forever (Hebrews 13:8). These are opportunities to cling to truths such as these (and many more):

> *"For as the heavens are higher than the earth, so are my ways higher than your ways and my thoughts than your thoughts"* (Isa. 55:9).

> *"The steadfast love of the Lord never ceases; his mercies never come to an end; they are new every morning; great is your faithfulness. 'The Lord is my portion,' says my soul, therefore I will hope in him'"* (Lam. 3:22-24).

> *"No good thing does he withhold from those who walk uprightly"* (Psa. 84:11b).

> *"Oh, fear the Lord, you his saints, for those who fear him have no lack! The young lions suffer want and hunger; but those who seek the Lord lack no good thing"* (Psa. 34:9,10).

> *"Be still, and know that I am God"* (Psa. 46:10).

I will admit that when I look back on old journals, I feel multiple emotions: some weary over repetitive petitions and desperate prayers, some grateful over answered prayers, and some amazed at the Shepherd's hand and the story the Lord has brought me thus far. Overall, I'm grateful for the union we have in Christ, for the years of recorded prayers I am able to look back on, and that He has answered my ultimate prayer, which is that I would "hunger and thirst for righteousness" (Matt. 5:6).

Chapter 10
What about fasting?

For several millennia, biblical fasting has meant abstaining from food for spiritual purposes. Indeed, fasting is mentioned at least forty times throughout the Bible, in both the Old and New Testaments.

Abstaining from food—an essential source of nourishment—is a path for drawing nearer to God or asking God to accomplish something profound in your life or the life of others. It is designed to allow you to get to know God more intimately.

After Jesus was baptized by John the Baptist, the Holy Spirit immediately led Him into the desert for forty days, where Jesus abstained from food and water. At the end of that time, when Jesus was famished as a human being, Satan tempted Him in three ways: the lust of the eyes, the lust of the flesh, and the pride of life. Jesus resisted all three temptations through the word of God.

Significantly, Jesus reversed what our ancestral parents fell prey to—Satan used the same three temptations on Adam and Eve, who succumbed, sinning against God. You can be confident that Jesus spent those forty days and forty nights in prayer to His Father, knowing what was coming. I believe that the length of the fasting by Jesus showed that He was not relying on anything other than the Father's actions through trusting in the word of God.

Over the years, fasting has moved partly away from just abstaining from food and water to other things special to that person. Fasting proves to God that you're serious about your concerns, prayers, and dependence on him. You have a better chance of hearing God when you're not concerned about your creature comforts. Besides prayer, fasting may lead you to search for scriptures. Honestly, it is not about abstaining from food; it's about feeding the heart of the believer.

Retired Baptist minister John Piper, who founded the Desiring God web-based ministry (desiringgod.org), writes, *"Christian fasting, at its root, is the hunger of a homesickness for God. Christian fasting is not only the spontaneous effect of superior satisfaction in God, it is also a chosen weapon against every force in the world that would take that satisfaction away."* Do you see that in Jesus' forty days of fasting?

In Jesus' early ministry, His disciples and followers did not fast. But Jesus spoke about fasting in the future:

> *"Can you make wedding guests fast while the bridegroom is with them? The days will come when the bridegroom is taken away from them, and they will fast in those days"* (Luke 5:33,34).

Jesus said these words when the Pharisees, who saw the disciples of John the Baptist fasting and offering prayers, asked why Jesus' disciples did not. Even the disciples of the Pharisees fasted.

Jesus spoke very clearly about the methodology of fasting:

> *"And when you fast do not look gloomy like the hypocrites, for they disfigure their faces that their fasting may be seen by others. Truly, I say to you, they have received their reward. But when you fast, anoint your head and wash your face, that your fasting may not be seen by others but by your Father who is in secret. And your Father who sees you in secret will reward you"* (Mt. 6:16-18).

In other words, you're not to go around with that "woe is me" look on your face and stooped shoulders, telling everyone that you're fasting. Fasting is meant to only be between you and God. However, collective fasting can occur within your family, church, Bible study group, or ministry.

Today, fasting by Christians is most common during the 40 days of Lent, the season of spiritual preparation before Easter. Lent is based on the 40 days of Jesus fasting in the wilderness and the 40 years of the Israelites wandering in the desert. In Western civilization, it begins on Ash Wednesday. Many Christians observe Lent through fasting (or moderation), repentance, self-denial, and spiritual discipline. The purpose is to deeply reflect on Jesus Christ and consider His suffering and sacrifice—His life, death, burial, and resurrection.

CHAPTER 10 - WHAT ABOUT FASTING?

Turning to the Old Testament, Isaiah writes about how the Israelites were oppressing their people by withholding wages from the workers and that God did not want the people to go a day without food. Instead, Isaiah says God wants the Israelites to abstain from the ways they've oppressed each other:

> *"If you do away with the yoke of oppression, with the pointing finger and malicious talk, and if you spend yourselves on behalf of the hungry and satisfy the needs of the oppressed, then your light will rise in the darkness, and your night will become like the noonday"* (Isa. 58:9-10 NIV).

In this case, "fasting" referred to refraining from denying food to the workers.

There are some basic steps to fasting. To me, the preparation of the heart and the purpose within our heart are essential. One of the most poignant verses in all of scripture, while not directly referring to fasting, is 2 Chronicles 7.14; I've highlighted the pertinent part in bold.

> *"Thus Solomon finished the house of the Lord and the king's house. All that Solomon had planned to do in the house of the Lord and in his own house he successfully accomplished. Then the Lord appeared to Solomon in the night and said to him: 'I have heard your prayer and have chosen this place for myself as a house of sacrifice. When I shut up the heavens so that there is no rain, or command the locust to devour the land, or send pestilence among my people,* **if my people who are called by my name humble themselves, and pray and seek my face and turn from their wicked ways, then I will hear from heaven and will forgive their sin and heal their land'"** (vv.11-14).

This speaks to the power of prayer and fasting. God will move heaven and earth to fulfill His promise to His people and the covenant that He has made in the blood of Jesus Christ. As a side note, a few years ago, the Lord led me to write a book, Revival of Repentance, based entirely on 2 Chronicles 7.14.

Fasting appears a few times in Moses' life. Consider, for example, Deuteronomy 9:9-11, when God called Moses to the mountain as he led the people from Egypt. For forty days, Moses did not eat or drink. He had no idea what God was planning. The Israelites were turning away from God, and Moses was perplexed.

He was the intermediary, like Jesus, between the Israelites and God. At the end of the forty days, God produced the Ten Commandments on two stone tablets, one of the most significant events in the Old Testament or biblical history.

Later, when Moses came down from the mountain and saw the sinfulness of the Israelites, he threw down the tablets and broke them, prostrated himself on the ground, and again spent forty days with no food or water, praying for God not to destroy all of them. God relented (Deut. 9:17-19). Soon after that, the Israelites again provoked the Lord to wrath. Moses once again lay prostrate before the Lord for forty days and forty nights because the Lord had said He would once again destroy the Israelites. God spared them again (Deut. 9:25-29).

What follows is that God commanded Moses to cut two new tablets for the same Ten Commandments. At God's invitation, Moses went to the mountain. So, because of Moses' intercession through prayer and fasting, we have the Ten Commandments today.

In the New Testament, we are shown the value of and results from fasting and prayer:

> *Mark 9:29 "And he said to them, 'This kind cannot be driven out by anything but prayer and fasting'"* (Mark 9:29).

Here, Jesus is conversing with His disciples about why they cannot cast out an unclean spirit from a boy. And this was Jesus' response. He's essentially saying that spiritual battles must be fought with spiritual weapons. (Note: Some translations do not include fasting, only prayer.)

> *"While they were worshiping the Lord and fasting, the Holy Spirit said, 'Set apart for me Barnabas and Saul for the work to which I have called them.' Then after fasting and praying they laid their hands on them and sent them off"* (Acts 13:2,3).

> *"And when they had appointed elders for them in every church, with prayer and fasting they committed them to the Lord in whom they had believed"* (Acts 14:23).

CHAPTER 10 - WHAT ABOUT FASTING?

> *"She [Anna, a prophetess] did not depart from the temple, worshiping with fasting and prayer night and day"* (Luke 2:37).

These three isolated instances brought about significant results and victories for God's kingdom, the latter being confirmation of Jesus' identity. While being presented in the temple for purification, Simeon and Anna bore witness that Jesus was the long-awaited Messiah and the light for the revelation to the Gentiles.

> *"And coming up at that very hour she began to give thanks to God and to speak of him to all who were waiting for the redemption of Jerusalem"* (Luke 2:38).

Daniel and his friends had been brought to Babylon by Nebuchadnezzar. He was faithful to God, which created a problem when Daniel did not worship the idol set up by the Babylonians. In prison, he asked the jailer to allow him to fast by not eating the food of the Babylonians for ten days but being allowed to eat food set out in the Jewish food laws to honor God. The jailer hesitantly agreed, and in the end, Daniel was healthier and stronger than the Babylonian young men. When brought before Nebuchadnezzar, the scripture says:

> *"And in every matter of wisdom and understanding about which the king inquired of them, he found them ten times better than all the magicians and enchanters that were in all his kingdom. And Daniel was there until the first year of King Cyrus"* (Dan. 1:20).

Daniel and his friends' prayers, fasting, and obedience honored God, who blessed them.

For a first-hand account of the value of fasting in Christian growth, turn the page to read Bosco Ruhinda's testimony of his journey from childhood to now. As you do, reflect on your own experience with fasting. Perhaps you can embrace this approach in your own spiritual journey.

Testimony by Jean Bosco Ruhinda

Founder of Trinitas Community Organization (TRICO), Kigali, Rwanda

"A Testament of My Life Built on Prayer"

I am Rwandan by nationality, but I was born as a refugee in Uganda, where life was extremely difficult. I was born into the poorest community, and even the poorest of people called us poor. I was born in a world marked by constant change and uncertainty; I found solace and strength in the age-old practice of prayer. This collection of testimonies aims to illuminate the profound impact of a life built on prayer, showcasing narratives that span diverse experiences, cultures, and backgrounds. From moments of despair to triumphs of the human spirit, my story attests to the enduring power of prayer in shaping, sustaining, and transforming lives.

A. The root cause of my life of prayer

In 2000, my country was still in a time of darkness following the tragedy of genocide against the Tutsi in 1994. My family had no hope for the future, and life was hard. Even getting daily bread was a miracle to us after trying many ways to survive, but there was no hope. I remember one night, my mum told me that I was useless, I had water in my head, and I would be a slave to my brothers. I went to bed that night and shook my head, feeling full of water. I automatically believed that lie, and from that night, I started to fight a battle to see how water could be removed from my head. The next day, I went to school, and they gave us a test, and I got zero out of ten. I took that as a sign confirming what my mum said about me and that I was going to be enslaved to my brothers and sister.

I remember waking at 3 a.m. that same week full of tears, broken-hearted, crying to the Almighty God, and trying to surrender my life to him, but I didn't know how to get saved. The following Sunday, I went to church, and my heart was hungry to receive Christ as the last option in my life. The motivation behind this was…if I receive Jesus, then He will remove the water in my head. I promised Him that if He could do that, I would serve Him for the rest of my entire life.

My prayer life started by reading the books of Psalms and Proverbs. I began dedicating myself to prayer and fasting because my heart was thirsty for the Lord. The more I kept on reading, the more He was quenching my thirst for Him. This pushed me to develop a habit of spending every morning in prayer and reading the Bible. I also decided to do praying and fasting every Wednesday of the week. I lived this kind of life for five years, from 2001 to 2006, when I was in high school. God anointed me at that time when I became a student union pastor, leading more than 1,200 students to Christ during that time.

B. Overcoming doubt

For five years, I had a battlefield in my mind trying to overcome the negative thoughts about who I was, trying to understand my identity in Christ, and winning over the negative words that were planted in me by my mother of thinking that I am useless. In 2006, when finishing high school, I began facing real life outside school. This caused me to spend three days praying and fasting without food, asking God the way to go. I decided that where He would lead me, I would follow, but I would not move if He did not move because my life was totally surrendered to trust the highest God.

During my prayers, the only voice that kept coming was…serve me, serve me, serve me!!! I remember having replied, "I will not be a pastor, I will not be a pastor, I will not be a pastor!" because I thought being a pastor was to be poor, and I was fighting not to be poor due to the life I was born into. Having become a pastor, I understand well the pain of living a life of luck.

C. Finding comfort

After that prayer, I remember asking God three things before I became a pastor:

1. Give me access to education: I wanted to study, but my family could not cover my basic needs, and I wanted God to give me more than

enough in terms of education. I wanted to be a smart pastor who understands what he is preaching.

2. Give me access to money: I wanted God to kill the spirit of poverty in me and my next generation and to start seeing money as a tool to serve him, not for luxury.

3. Give me access to nations: My heart was to take the gospel to all nations because I was burdened for the lost. That's why I requested Him to grant me nations.

Prayer is not wasting time but investing time. God started answering my prayers by testing me. He gave me those promises, but He moved me from promises to problems, from problems to provision. I kept on building my life into a prayer lifestyle, and I decided to start spending 40 days of prayers and fasting every year to seek more of His face, not asking things but creating a heart of depending more on Jesus.

D. My business life and prayer

In 2009, I started my first business and failed; I started another one in 2010 and failed. After that, I decided to stay in my room for one month, praying and fasting, asking God to show me my vision of 40 years to come. I remember at around 2 a.m. on the last day, when I was reading my Bible, full of passion and waiting upon the Lord, I heard a voice say…

> *"I will give you the treasures of darkness and hidden riches of secret places, That you may know that I, the LORD, Who call you by your name, Am the God of Israel"* (Isa. 45:3 NKJV).

Then my eyes were opened, I kept praying, and I heard a voice telling me again…

> *"Thus says the LORD, your Redeemer, the Holy One of Israel: 'I am the LORD your God, who teaches you to profit, who leads you in the way you should go'"* (Isa. 48:17 ESV).

Then, my mind opened to Him until the voice told me that the Father, the Son, and the Holy Spirit would be my partner. That is where I got the name Trinitas for my business and non-profit.

Then God showed me the four phases of my life:

Phase one, from age 25 to 35: Trial Phase
Phase two, from age 35 to 45: Build People
Phase three, from age 45 to 55: Build a Legacy
Phase four, from age 55 to 65: Invest in Young People

I praise God for prayer.

VICTORY THROUGH PRAYER!

Chapter 11
Blessings and Benedictions

Without getting too theological, it's important to grasp the meaning of both of these words in secular and biblical terms. Blessing is defined as *"the act or words of one that blesses"* or *"a thing conducive to happiness or welfare."* Benediction is *"a short invocation for divine health, blessing, and guidance, usually at the end of worship service or ceremony."*

Blessings

The Hebrew word most often translated as *"bless"* is *barak*, which can mean to *praise, congratulate, or salute*. This is used in Genesis at the creation. At the end of the fifth day, God pronounced a blessing on every living creature, those in the waters, and every winged bird:

"And God saw that it was good. And God blessed them, saying, 'Be fruitful and multiply and fill the waters in the seas, and let birds multiply on the earth'" (Gen. 1:21b,22).

Then came the final day of God's creation work. Day six is when He created man.

"So God created man in his own image, in the image of God he created him; male and female he created them. And God blessed them. And God said to them, "Be fruitful and multiply and fill the earth and subdue it, and have dominion over the fish of the sea and over the birds of the heavens and over every living thing that moves on the earth"' (Gen. 1:27,28).

These are the first recordings of blessings in scripture. God has dominion in the heavens and was transferring the dominion on Earth to His created beings. He didn't just create everything and tell Adam and Eve to have a good time and check back every now and then so He could see how they were doing. That would have been senseless. The blessing was the power, the authority, and the instruction for what His creations were to do. They had God's authority and blessing to accomplish it. God was literally breathing life and personal purpose into them.

Because God had given man authority, He also gave him the privilege and authority to pronounce blessings. Two examples come to mind.

First is the blessing of the patriarch in Genesis 12:1-3, when God promises to bless Abram (later Abraham), make his name great, and, through him, bless all the families of the Earth. When Abraham's son Isaac was old, he called his two sons, Esau and Jacob, to pronounce the blessing on the older Esau. However, through Isaac's wife Rebecca's scheme, Jacob received the blessing according to God's sovereign plan.

The second example involves Jacob (whose name was changed by God to Israel). He eventually had twelve sons, who became the twelve tribes of Israel. When Jacob was old, he called his sons together and stated the qualities of each one—some good, some not so good. Only Joseph received Jacob's blessing (Gen. 49:22-25).

Joseph was then betrayed by his brothers, who, out of jealousy of their father, sold him into slavery. Because of Jacob's (aka God's) blessing, Joseph not only endured many major trials, but he also became second in command under Pharaoh in Egypt. In the time of famine, when his brothers came to Egypt in search of food, Joseph tested them and eventually saved them as well as the entire family of Israel (Jacob), which numbered seventy. Four hundred-plus years later, the twelve tribes left for the Promised Land with more than one million people. Joseph was a foreshadow of Jesus.

Fast forward to Jesus' baptism when He was 30 years old by John the Baptist. When Jesus came up out of the water, the Holy Spirit, in the image of a dove, descended upon him, and God pronounced a blessing on His Son before Jesus' three years of ministry, death on the cross, resurrection from the grave, and ascension back to heaven. This was the Father's spoken blessing:

> *"And when Jesus was baptized, immediately he went up from the water, and behold, the heavens were opened to him, and he saw the Spirit of God descending like a dove and coming to rest on him; and behold, a*

CHAPTER 11 - BLESSINGS AND BENEDICTIONS

voice from heaven said, 'This is my beloved Son with whom I am well pleased'" (Mt. 3:16,17).

We are told that Jesus was led immediately into the wilderness without food or water for forty days and was tempted by Satan by the lust of the eyes, the lust of the flesh, and the pride of life. These were the same temptations that Eve and Adam had succumbed to. Jesus, however, defeated each temptation with the word of God.

These Biblical accounts demonstrate the power of the blessing. Reflect on what it meant for Abraham, Jacob, Joseph, and Jesus, who received a second blessing from His Father on the Mount of Transfiguration, the day before His crucifixion.

In the New Testament, especially in the book of Acts, blessings are accompanied by prayer, fasting, the laying on of hands, and anointing people for mission and healing. The following are but a few instances,

> *"While they were worshiping the Lord and fasting, the Holy Spirit said, 'Set apart for me Barnabas and Saul for the work to which I have called them.' Then after fasting and praying they laid their hands on them and sent them off"* (Acts 13:2,3).

> *"'Truly, I say to you, whoever does not receive the kingdom of God like a child shall not enter it.' And he [Jesus] took them in his arms and blessed them, laying his hands on them"* (Mark 10:15,16).

> *"These they set before the apostles, and they prayed and laid hands on them"* (Acts 6:6).

> *"While they were worshiping the Lord and fasting, the Holy Spirit said, 'Set apart for me Barnabas and Saul for the work to which I have called them.' Then, after fasting and praying, they laid their hands on them and sent them off"* (Acts 13:2,3).

> *"And he laid his hands on her, and immediately she was made straight, and she glorified God"* (Luke 13:13).

As a father, grandfather, and now a great-grandfather, I strongly encourage every father to perform a prayer of blessing over all newborn children in the family. And to encourage your sons and sons-in-law, and your grandsons and grand sons-in-law to do the same for their children. I suggest that when the family is gathered on the first day or two after the birth, you place your hand on the head of this child and dedicate it to the Lord, prayerfully giving the child back to the Lord as it is his.

On every grandchild's sixth birthday, I claim a life verse in scripture for them, print it on an 8-by-10 photographic portrait, and frame it for them. It's another way to bless the next generation. Each year, I also prepare a poem of blessing from the first to the eighteenth birthday, then the twenty-first birthday, and at their rehearsal dinner. Verbal and written blessings are both very special. I offer these as inspiration to choose your own methods of blessing, with God as your guide.

Benedictions

Benedictions are seen throughout scripture as godly prayers of blessing for many purposes. I encourage you to memorize a few passages to use when God's Spirit prompts you to offer a benediction in your daily life.

Here's an example from my own experience leading a series of fatherhood trainings in prisons and in the marketplace. At the conclusion, I ask the participants to circle around me in prayer. Then I walk around with my hand held high as if anointing their head and offer a prayer of blessing and a specific benediction on each man. Specifically, I am asking Christ, through the Holy Spirit, to ensure their success moving forward. They have now been equipped to lead their family well, and this is their benediction of blessing.

The following select verses are a good place to start:

> "The Lord spoke to Moses, saying, 'Speak to Aaron and his sons, saying, Thus you shall bless the people of Israel: you shall say to them, The Lord bless you and keep you; the Lord make his face to shine upon you and be gracious to you; the Lord lift up his countenance upon you and give you peace'" (Num. 6:22-26).

CHAPTER 11 - BLESSINGS AND BENEDICTIONS

"Come, bless the Lord, all you servants of the Lord, who stand by night in the house of the Lord! Lift up your hands to the holy place and bless the Lord! May the Lord bless you from Zion, he who made heaven and earth!" (Psa. 134).

"Peace I [Jesus] leave with you; my peace I give to you. Not as the world gives do I give to you. Let not your hearts be troubled, neither let them be afraid" (John 14:27).

"Now to him who is able to do far more abundantly than all that we ask or think, according to the power at work within us, to him be glory in the church and in Christ Jesus throughout all generations, forever and ever. Amen" (Eph. 3:20).

"May the God of hope fill you with all joy and peace in believing, so that by the power of the Holy Spirit you may abound in hope" (Rom.15:13).

"The grace of our Lord Jesus Christ and the love of God and the fellowship of the Holy Spirit be with you all" (2 Cor. 13:14).

"(May) the peace of God, which surpasses all understanding, will guard your hearts and your minds in Christ Jesus" (Phil. 4:7).

"And let the peace of Christ rule in your hearts, to which indeed you were called in one body. And be thankful" (Col. 3:15).

"May the God of endurance and encouragement grant you to live in such harmony with one another, in accordance with Christ Jesus, that together you may with one voice glorify the God and Father of our Lord Jesus Christ" (Rom. 15:5-6).

"Now may the God of peace himself sanctify you completely, and may your whole spirit and soul and body be kept blameless at the coming of our Lord Jesus Christ. He who calls you as faithful; he will surely do it" (I Thess. 5:23-24).

"Now may our Lord Jesus Christ himself, and God our Father, who loved us and gave us eternal comfort and good hope through grace, comfort your hearts and establish them in every good work and word" (2 Thess. 2:16-17).

"To the King of ages, immortal, invisible, the only God, be honor and glory forever and ever. Amen" (I Tim. 1:17).

"Now may the God of peace who brought again from the dead our Lord Jesus, the great shepherd of the sheep, by the blood of the eternal covenant, equip you with everything good that you may do his will, working in us that which is pleasing in his sight, through Jesus Christ, to whom be glory forever and ever. Amen" (Heb. 13:20-21).

"But grow in the grace and knowledge of our Lord and Savior Jesus Christ. To him be the glory both now and to the day of eternity. Amen" (2 Pet. 3:18).

"Now to him who is able to keep you from stumbling and to present you blameless before the presence of his glory with great joy, to the only God, our Savior, through Jesus Christ our Lord, be glory, majesty, dominion, and authority, before all time and now and forever. Amen" (Jude 24,25).

Blessings and benedictions incorporate the heart's desire for worship, empowerment, and anointing. They capture the very essence of praise. As the anointed word of God through the power of the Holy Spirit, they allow us to express what we cannot on our own. Family, friends, church members, missionaries, pastors, teachers, ministry workers—all these and more need our blessings and benedictions. What a privilege God has given us.

Chapter 12
Before we say "Amen!"

The following are random thoughts about prayer. These are some of my experiences over the years that did not fit into the previous chapters.

It is important to imagine and embrace the fact that you're not just praying alone; this applies as well when praying with a small group, in a church congregation, or at a prayer conference. Your prayers are being joined with a multitude of prayers from all over the world, some of which are very similar to yours—maybe nearly identical—and they all rise as a sweet aroma to the Father. So, don't mistakenly think you or your group's prayers are in a vacuum. You are a part of a host of men and women and children praying. There is assured victory in that.

Here's a great set of truths to be encouraged by:

> *"Truly, I say to you, whatever you bind on earth shall be bound in heaven, and whatever you loose on earth shall be loosed in heaven. Again I say to you, if two of you agree on earth about anything they ask, it will be done for them by my Father in heaven. For where two or three are gathered in my name, there am I among them"*
> (Mt. 18:18-20).

Sabbaticals are a gift from God. Let's start with its meaning: *"Of or appropriate to the sabbath."* It's a time of rest. God rested on the seventh day after creating everything. He set the Sabbath, or the seventh day of the week, as a day of rest. For most of the Christian Church throughout the world, it falls on Sunday. But sabbaticals can vary from several hours each day for a period of time to a full day, week, month, or year. A prayer sabbatical is a time to get alone with your Bible, God's word, and your thoughts.

When taking an extended sabbatical for prayer away from home, you are encouraged to leave all technology behind and to bring enough food and water, a change of clothes, your Bible, a listening ear and open heart, a journal, and nothing else. The goal is not to encounter anyone else. It's an intimate time for just you and the Lord.

Prayer walks are another common way to commune with God. Depending on your objective, they can be as simple as strolling through your neighborhood, praying for every home you pass. You could focus your prayer walks by carving off several blocks at a time.

Several years ago, a friend and I felt led to pray for the City of Dallas. After a time of prayer together, asking God for direction, we went to the city limits on the north, south, east, and west. At each place, we spent time anointing the city for God, asking Him to do great and mighty things—to bless the leaders, the churches, the saved and unsaved, and so much more.

One significant prayer walk happened several decades ago in the 75212 West Dallas neighborhood. The area was experiencing extreme poverty, with very few amenities or infrastructure. It was as if the city leaders had abandoned it despite being very near and in clear view of the central business district of Dallas. It was so close yet seemingly far apart.

Meanwhile, as a young man, Arrvel Wilson had moved away and joined the Marines. He had little desire to ever return. But something happened. His father, who had long been a believer, did a prayer walk around the perimeter of the area, claiming the community for God. A few years later, Arrvel was led by the Lord to return to West Dallas with his wife, Eletha. God started using them in a mighty way to be the vessels bringing dynamic change to this community.

Soon after, several North Dallas churches started adopting the area for mission work, and Arrvel himself started and pastored the West Dallas Community Church, which spawned West Dallas Community School. Mercy Street Dallas and several other ministries were birthed to meet the needs of the community. Ballfields were developed, and a new YMCA opened. Businesses relocated here and created job opportunities. It is now a thriving community. One would have to believe that the prayer walk by Mr. Wilson decades ago honoring God was the catalyst for the transformation of this West Dallas community.

Please remember that this book has been written from the heart and experience

CHAPTER 12 - BEFORE WE SAY "AMEN!"

of a man who has made many, many mistakes over my 86 years on Earth. I have experienced the love, forgiveness, discipline, grace, and mercy of our Lord. The life, death, burial, resurrection, and ascension of Jesus provide victory through prayer until HE returns. Hallelujah!

I've chosen James, the half-brother of Jesus, to close us with his well-crafted prayer of faith. It expresses the breadth and depth of a man who knew Christ and the power of prayer.

> *"Is anyone among you suffering? Let him pray. Is there anyone cheerful? Let him sing praise. Is anyone among you sick? Let him call for the elders of the church, and let them pray over him, anointing him with oil in the name of the Lord. And the prayer of faith will save the one who is sick, and the Lord will raise him up. And if he has committed sins, he will be forgiven. Therefore, confess your sins to one another and pray for one another, that you may be healed. The prayer of a righteous person has great power as it is working. Elijah was a man with a nature like ours, and he prayed fervently that it might not rain, and for three years and six months it did not rain on the earth. Then he prayed again, and heaven gave rain, and the earth bore its fruit. My brothers, if anyone among you wanders from the truth and someone brings him back, let him know that whoever brings back a sinner from his wandering will save his soul from death and will cover a multitude of sins"* (James 5:13-20).

That's a prayer of victory! I now dedicate all that has been shared in this book to the glory of God the Father, in the name of Jesus, and in the power of the Holy Spirit. Amen and amen!

Testimony by Will Ellerman
(as voiced and scribed)
Prayer Warrior

Prayer means to be humble. To be a wise man. To listen and obey because I do want to live for Him. Prayer helps me be engaged with Him. And He encourages me and gives me strength.

Prayer is to have the fullness of God. Prayer is to think hard about what is true. To listen to His Word and to know the Bible and what He is telling us. To not look back or lose heart. To be awakened in me; to light up in me.

Because Jesus taught us to pray. He's our Faithful God. He has greater things that He wants to do. He is the foundation of the world. He makes good things for us. He gives us grace. It is right to do what is good for us. He gives us light and salvation. He brings us near to Him. He is the Sovereign LORD. He still watches over us. He always protects us. He's the Son of God.

Prayer is good for us. It helps me know Him better. To not waste time; to bring beauty from ashes. To give us hope and a future. To love one another. To be kind to our neighbor. To keep us safe from the evil one. He is our shield and our buckler.

I open His Word and pray to our Father. I feel His Love for me. I feel close to Him. He has made us well for our soul, mind, and strength. He is our King. He gives us new jobs to do. I ask God to forgive my sins and cast out my fears. He wants me to rejoice in His Name.

I like to pray because "I am fearfully and wonderfully made. Wonderful are Your works; my soul knows it very well" (Psa. 139:13-14). I pray for others because I care about them. I do hear His voice. And He is calling to me and telling me what He is doing. And He's all around me. From the top of my head to the soul of my feet and all parts in between. I am His faithful servant, and I am His workmanship. I am His child. I am God's warrior. I want to tell the truth. I don't have to be anxious about my life. His prayers are inside my heart. I ask God to have mercy on me. To be rooted and grounded in His Love. To not be anxious. To have joy and confidence. To bear much fruit.

Chapter 13
The gospel and prayer for salvation

Hopefully, you have enjoyed reading the preceding chapters and testimonies and were challenged and blessed by all or some of the material. But we should never lose sight of the overwhelming evidence that the Source and Author of all life is God, the Creator. His only Son, Jesus Christ, was there in the beginning with the Father and the Holy Spirit. Old and New Testament scriptures speak clearly about this matter.

In John 1:3, the apostle tells us, *"All things were made through him, and without him was not any thing made that was made."* John goes on to say in verse 4, *"In him was life, and the life was the light of men."*

Hebrews 1:1,2 tells us, *"God…in these last days he has spoken to us by his Son, whom he appointed the heir of all things, through whom also he created the world."*

Jesus also says of himself in John 14.6, *"I am the way, and the truth, and the life. No one comes to the Father except through me."*

All God's creation speaks of His eternal qualities and majesty. We have but to gaze at the miracles of life each day to see and be reminded of them. Maybe for the first time, or in a deeper devotion, you drew near to God through the moments you read and pondered on His word. Possibly, He spoke specifically to you, and there is now a desire to know Him more intimately.

As God said through His servant James, *"Draw near to God and he will draw near to you"* (James 4:8).

How does one do that?

First, know that the gospel, according to 1 Corinthians 15:1-5, is summed up in ten words: *"Christ died for our sins and rose from the dead."*

The Roman road leading to salvation is provided in the following verses:

> Romans 3:23: *"For all have sinned and fall short of the glory of God."*

> Romans 6:23: *"For the wages of sin is death, but the free gift of God is eternal life in Christ Jesus our Lord."*

> Romans 5:8: *"But God shows his love for us in that while we were still sinners, Christ died for us."*

> Ephesians 2:8,9: *"For by grace you have been saved through faith. And this is not your own doing; it is the gift of God, not a result of works, so that no one may boast."*

In John 5:24, we see a truth that can be embraced through faith (trust) in Jesus who tells you and me, *"Truly, truly, I say to you, whoever hears my word and believes him who sent me <u>has eternal life</u>. He does not come into judgment, but <u>has passed</u> from death to <u>life</u>"* [underlined for emphasis].

Jesus spoke clearly again in John 11:25 when He said, *"I am the resurrection and the life. Whoever believes in me, though he die, yet shall he live."*

If it is the desire of your heart to trust Jesus Christ for your salvation and partake in His eternal life, then the following prayer is a suggested way for you to take the step today. Read over the prayer, and if it reflects your heart's desire, then pray it right now. Know that it is not the prayer that saves but placing your trust in Christ alone for your salvation.

> "Dear God, I know I'm a sinner. I know my sin deserves to be punished. I believe Christ died for me and rose from the grave. I trust you, Jesus, alone as my Savior. Thank you for the forgiveness of my sins and the everlasting life that I now have. In Jesus' name, amen."

Welcome to the kingdom of God! Did you hear the angels rejoicing? Well, they are!

CHAPTER 13 - THE GOSPEL AND PRAYER FOR SALVATION

Eternal life is based on fact, not feeling. *Now…*

1. Tell God what is on your mind through prayer (Philippians 4:6,7).

2. Read the Bible daily (according to 2 Timothy 3:16,17). Start in the book of Philippians or John.

3. Worship with God's people in a local Christ-centered church (Hebrews 10:24,25).

4. Tell others about Jesus Christ (Matthew 4:19).

The best place to start praying is with your family. You might even discover they have been praying for you for some time. Rejoice together and go and enjoy the abundant life that comes with abiding, both in the Lord, in the home, and beyond. Read John 15:1-12 alone and with your family. You will gain great insight into your new life of abiding in Christ.

I'll end with my personal prayer for every reader who has trusted Christ for their salvation.

> "Father God, I rejoice that your Son was willing to sacrifice His life as a ransom for many. You have provided this grace to allow men and women, even children, to come to a saving knowledge of Jesus Christ and to receive eternal life. Lord, guide those who have trusted you, giving them the assurance that you will never leave them nor forsake them. Be glorified through their lives. Help them to be ambassadors for Christ and your kingdom all the days of their lives. We thank you for your love, your mercy, and your grace. In Jesus' name, amen."

I recommend taking the time to write out your experience in this journey through the *Victory Through Prayer!* book and your moment of salvation. After you're through with the book, pass it on to someone you wish to bless through prayer.

VICTORY THROUGH PRAYER!

Prayer Quotes

Quotes about prayer can be incredibly helpful in our everyday lives. Many that we memorize or refer to often prompt us to do things that we might not be motivated to do otherwise. I chose the following selections because I believe they help us better understand the true power and essence of prayer in God's kingdom.

"If prayer is anything, then it is everything." Puritan Pastor

"Prayer lays hold of God's plan and becomes the link between His will and its accomplishment on earth. Amazing things happen, and we are given the privilege of being the channels of the Holy Spirit's prayer." Elisabeth Elliot

"True prayer is a way of life, not just for use in cases of emergency. Make it a habit, and when the need arises you will be in practice." Billy Graham

"Is prayer your steering wheel or your spare tire?" Corrie Ten Boom

"To be a Christian without prayer is no more possible than to be alive without breathing." Martin Luther

"True prayer is neither a mere mental exercise nor a vocal performance. It is far deeper than that—it is spiritual transaction with the Creator of Heaven and Earth." Charles Spurgeon

"Prayer is not only asking, but an attitude of mind which produces the atmosphere in which asking is perfectly natural." Oswald Chambers

"Our prayers may be awkward. Our attempt may be feeble. But since the power of prayer is in the one who hears it and not in the one who says it, our prayers do make a difference." Max Lucado

"Pray until you pray." Puritan Pastor

"Prayer is not asking. Prayer is putting oneself in the hands of God, at His disposition, and listening to His voice in the depths of our hearts." Mother Teresa

"Our praying needs to be pressed and pursued with an energy that never tires, a persistency which will not be denied, and a courage that never fails." E.M. Bounds

"When faith ceases to pray, it ceases to live." E.M. Bounds

"Four things let us ever keep in mind: God hears prayer, God heeds prayer, God answers prayer, and God delivers by prayer." E.M. Bounds

"When a Christian shuns fellowship with other Christians, the devil smiles, when he stops studying the Bible, the devil laughs. When he stops praying, the devil shouts for joy." Corrie Ten Boom

"Don't worry about having the right words; worry more about having the right heart. It's not eloquence he seeks, just honesty." Max Lucado

"Every great movement of God can be traced to a kneeling figure." Dwight L. Moody

"To pray is to accept that we are, and always will be, wholly dependent on God for everything." Tim Keller

"Prayer is the way you defeat the devil, reach the lost, restore a backslider, strengthen the saints, send missionaries out, cure the sick, accomplish the impossible, and know the will of God." David Jeremiah

"Prayer is the vital breath of the Christian; not the thing that makes him alive, but the evidence that he is alive." Oswald Chambers

"None can believe how powerful prayer is, and what it is able to effect, but those who have learned it by experience." Martin Luther

"The value of consistent prayer is not that He will hear us, but that we will hear Him." William J. McGill

> *"Prayer honors God, acknowledges His being, exalts His power, adores His providence, secures His aid."* E. M. Bounds

> *"Grant that I may not pray alone with the mouth; help me that I may pray from the depths of my heart."* Martin Luther

> *"The greatest tragedy of life is not unanswered prayer, but unoffered prayer."* F.B. Meyer

> *"It matters little what form of prayer we adopt or how many words we use. What matters is the faith which lays hold on God, knowing that He knows our needs before we even ask Him. That is what gives Christian prayer its boundless confidence and its joyous certainty."* Dietrich Bonhoeffer

These words of wisdom are just a taste of the conviction and practice of these great "warriors for Christ." What they have experienced in their lives and in the world in which they have ministered is profound. The sayings all point to the incredible power of prayer, too—and should encourage us to go and do likewise.

What I hear is clear: *"Pray without ceasing!"* It's not a "one-and-done" act; it's a lifestyle. It is like breathing in and breathing out. Everything starts and ends with prayer. I have always believed prayer is a parent's most important tool in their toolbox.

I'll close this section with the words of Paul to the Philippians:

> *"The Lord is at hand; do not be anxious about anything, but in everything by prayer and supplication with thanksgiving let your requests be made known to God. And the peace of God, which surpasses all understanding, will guard your hearts and your minds in Christ Jesus"* (Phil. 4:5b-7).

And his exhortation to Timothy:

> *"First of all, then, I urge that supplications, prayers, intercessions, and thanksgivings be made for all people, for kings and all who are in*

high positions, that we may lead a peaceful and quiet life, godly and dignified in every way. This is good, and it is pleasing in the sight of God our Savior, who desires all people to be saved and to come to the knowledge of the truth. For there is one God, and there is one mediator between God and men, the man Christ Jesus, who gave himself as a ransom for all, which is the testimony given at the proper time"
(I Tim. 2:1-6).

Pray about everything, all in the name of Jesus Christ, our intercessor and mediator, in the power of the Holy Spirit. The Father will hear them all, and act accordingly. What a privilege we have here on Earth! *Victory is assured!!*

Seven Hebrew Words for Praise

Prayer need not always be a time of quietude or solemnity. The Old Testament has seven words that all mean praise—only one of them indicates restraint. Hallelujah!!!

1. HALAL: To jump, dance, to be loud and clamorous *(see Psalm 150:2)*.

2. YADAH: To throw your hands up and forward while making a confession about God *(see Isaiah 25:1)*.

3. TOWDAH: To lift your hands in thanksgiving *(see Psalm 107:22)*.

4. SHABACH: A loud, joyous shout of testimony *(see Psalm 145:4)*.

5. ZAMAR: To worship the Lord while playing an instrument *(see Psalm 98:4)*.

6. BARAK: To kneel in reverence and submission *(see Psalm 66:20)*.

7. TEHILLAH: To sing a spontaneous, unrehearsed song of the Lord, from your spirit *(see Psalm 22:3)*.

To dig deeper into the scriptural references, visit thewayoftheworshipper.com/seven-hebrew-words-for-praise.

Acknowledgements

I want to thank all those who contributed to this book. My daughter, Evelyn Battaglia, suggested it and edited the material, and my other daughter, Rebecca Ellerman, shared her prayer testimony, as did my grandchildren: Annie D'Spain, Sarah Peyton Ellerman, and Will Ellerman. My wife, Joanne, provided prayers and emotional support. Kurt Nelson wrote the Foreword, Dr. Ramesh Richard wrote an endorsement, and others shared their prayer testimonies, including (in alphabetical order) Robyn Bush, Prashant Joy, Bill Lamberth, Dr. Jeffrey Parker, Annie Roberson, David Rodriguez, John Roper, and Bosco Ruhinda. Mel Climer of Climer Design designed the book and JPS Books and Logistics published it. Ultimate thanks to the Lord, who, through His Holy Spirit, inspired and guided the writing of the content.

About the Author

In 1986, author Bill C. Dotson founded Dallas Real Estate Ministries (DREM) and served as its Executive Director. In 2011, Bill founded *Abiding Fathers* and served as President until 2023. He has authored and published six books and writes a weekly devotional called *Life* Today concerning life lessons from God's creation and addressing fatherhood. Bill lives in Dallas with his wife Joanne. They have two daughters, five grandchildren (two married), and five great-grandchildren.

VICTORY THROUGH PRAYER!